The British School at Athens

The First Hundred Years

by
Helen Waterhouse

THE BRITISH SCHOOL AT ATHENS
THAMES AND HUDSON
1986

Published by
The British School at Athens
31–34 Gordon Square, London WC1H 0PY

8800015981

Distributed by
Thames and Hudson
30 Bloomsbury Street, London WC1B 3QP

ISBN 0 500 96022 4

DF
11
.W28
1986

*The endpapers show an early plan
of the School garden and its trees*

*The dust jacket shows a late
nineteenth century view of the Acropolis
(Photo: Ashmolean Museum, Cast Gallery)*

Typeset at Oxford University Computing Centre
Printed in Great Britain
at the Alden Press
Oxford

Contents

Introduction

The main sources of this history have been the Minutes of the Managing Committee (the first volume of which is unfortunately missing) and the *Annual Report of the Managing Committee*. Extra matter has been provided by letters and diaries, lent or given by old students or their relatives, by reminiscences, often vivid and detailed, sent in generous response to my appeals, and by the readiness of former Directors to help; I am particularly indebted to Peter Megaw, Sinclair Hood and John Cook. Hector Catling, the present Director, has supplied the account of the Fitch Laboratory, which I felt unable to attempt. The same Directors supplied the text, or its basis, for the sections on excavations in Cyprus (Megaw, text), Chios (Hood, text), and Old Smyrna (basis, Cook), and John Boardman, to whose support and encouragement, and practical help, so much is owed, supplied the summary of the School's excavations overseas.

Much light on past periods has been shed by the published work of others, the *Letters and Light Verse* of R. Carr Bosanquet, published by his wife (1938), and her own *Late Harvest*; the *Aegean Memories* and *Greek Memories* of Compton Mackenzie; and three books by Dilys Powell, *The Traveller's Journey is done*, *The Villa Ariadne*, and *An Affair of the Heart*. Books about Sir Arthur Evans and Knossos are mentioned in the text.

Its occasion is the centenary of the School's founding, in 1886, an occasion for celebration certainly, but also for considering what contribution the School has made to the growth and development of archaeology and to the preservation of Greek studies, not in any chauvinistic spirit of competition with the achievements of other nationalities or institutions, but as a foundation on which to build. Through its students, the School has profoundly influenced the development in this country of every aspect of Hellenic studies. From the beginning they have moved back from Athens to work in universities and museums, to teach in colleges and schools, and in due course to send out a proportion of their pupils to become students in their turn. Their teaching (as far as books in English are concerned) has relied very largely on the published works of successive generations of School members. In recent years, a more conscious effort to promote Hellenic studies has been made by the summer courses for undergraduates and spring courses for classics teachers described below.

It has not been easy to decide to what audience this book shall be addressed, and the result is a compromise. Colleagues and *alumni* of all periods may find in it much that is commonplace and dull — 'surely everyone knows *that*'. Less specialised readers may find things taken for granted which might have merited explanation. To the former I would say that in writing I have learned a very great deal — the intentional absence of footnotes does not imply absence of research! — some of it surprising. To the latter I can only apologise.

The annals of the School will form the first part, giving as compendious a record of the hundred years as possible. Next, its London base will be explored, with what may seem to some an excessive emphasis on its finances. In fact, it is hard to overstate the part played by finance in shaping the School's development and the directions taken by the studies of its members. There will follow some account of the School as part of Athens, its buildings, its library and collections, its relationships in Greece. Knossos is treated separately, for, though an integral and important part of the School, its development has been different. Excavations, briefly mentioned in the annals, will be treated more broadly, and an attempt will be made to give some account in general terms of the other work of students. George Macmillan, writing a history of the quarter-century to 1911, was able to list some of the more important books written and positions held by former members; this is beyond the compass of an account of the full one hundred years. Finally, an attempt will be made to catch something of the quality of life at the School as people have remembered it; this lacks, sadly, almost all detail for the period before 1914 — too many 'founding fathers' were dead before the History was mooted — and has surprisingly little for the last dozen or so years, when the students have been, perhaps, too busy with active preoccupations to think their life-style worth recording.

A good institution has a life of its own, beyond its individual parts; the School in Athens has been called 'the best academic club in Europe'. To be part of it is to add to the privilege of living and working in Greece a secure base, professional standards not less rigorous for being tempered by good-fellowship, and a network of friendships and shared interests, across the generations, lasting often into old age.

It was a decision of the Managing Committee that this history should be written, and they have given free access to Minutes and files both in London and in Athens. Warm thanks are due to the Secretaries past and present, in London and in Athens, especially to Edith Clay, who has saved me many errors, and to Sally Bicknell and Elizabeth Waywell in London, who welcomed me in the Office, found and copied papers for me, and in many ways promoted and encouraged the project. Corrections and additions to a draft version were made with meticulous care by the Chairman, Robert Cook, his predecessor Peter Warren, by Peter Megaw, Sinclair Hood, and John Boardman; for parts of it the same office was performed by John Cook, Bernard Ashmole, Lisa French, Peter Fraser, Vronwy Hankey, Robert Hopper, Mervyn Popham, Lord William Taylour, and Richard Tomlinson. For interesting reminiscences I am most grateful to Helen Brock, R. H. Bulmer, Oliver Davies, Oliver Dickinson, John Graham, Nicholas Hammond, André Kenny,

David Lewis, Brian Sparkes and Frank Stubbings. Ann Brown's contribution to the early history of Knossos will be found in the relevant place. How much I have owed to Robin and Mary Burn, to Miriam Chandler for copying her sister Lilian's diary, and to Richard Lamb for copies of Winifred Lamb's letters will be apparent to the reader. To the Treasurer, who promoted it, and Hector Catling, who arranged it, I owe the pleasure and profit of a visit to the School in Athens and to Knossos in 1984; that it was not only business but a great pleasure was due not only to all the officials of the School in both places but to the students, whose welcome was both heart-warming and rejuvenating.

My thanks are owed to Mrs. Charles Bosanquet, Mr. David Bosanquet and Lady Hardman for permission to quote from their mother's books and to reproduce their photograph of R. Carr Bosanquet. Miss Penrose very kindly sent me the photograph of her grandfather; Sir Robin Mackworth Young went to much trouble to supply the photograph of his father. Most of the other portraits are copied from the Athens archive. Penny Wilson, Assistant Librarian, copied for me the illustrations from Heaton Comyn's book on the Penrose Library, and the plan of the School temenos used for our end-papers. Ken and Diana Wardle have been of the greatest assistance in providing good photographs of portraits and buildings at the School in Athens. Alan Peatfield and Christine Morris kindly took the views of the Taverna, the Villa Ariadne and the Stratigraphical Museum at Knossos.

Vronwy Hankey brought to my notice the important passages in the Journal of W. M. Flinders Petrie. For permission to quote from the Journal I am indebted to the Griffith Institute (Oxford), the Petrie Museum (in University College London) and, by the good office of Peggy Drower, to Miss Ann Petrie.

The School's journal, *Annual of the British School at Athens* is referred to in the text as *BSA*.

Chapter I

Prelude and Annals

Before embarking on the history of the British School itself, it may be well to survey briefly the circumstances in Greece and at home into which it was born. By the early nineteenth century travellers to Greece with a serious and scholarly approach had become numerous; their accounts of what they saw are still valuable today — one need only cite those of Colonel Martin Leake. After Greece became independent, regular missions of multi-disciplinary character were active; two of these, the *Expédition Scientifique de la Morée, 1831–38*, and Lebas and Landron's *Voyage archéologique en Grèce et Asie Mineure fait par ordre du Gouvernement Français, 1843–7*, may be regarded as ancestral to the foundation in 1846 of the first foreign school in Greece, the École Française d'Athènes, then and ever since an official body. There had been an Archaeological Institute in Rome, largely supported from Berlin, since 1829; to some extent this was an international body, and published its *Annali* in Italian. In 1843 the parent Prussian Institute began to publish in Berlin the *Archaeologische Zeitung* (ancestor of the *Jahrbuch*), with a wider scope. In 1874, renamed the Imperial Institute, it established another branch in Athens, with its own organ, the *Athenische Mitteilungen*, and began to excavate on a large scale at Olympia. In 1881 the American School of Classical Studies, a private body, opened its doors in Amalias Street.

In Britain, the Society of the Dilettanti, founded in 1732 as a prestigious dining club, soon showed itself to be the first coherent body to sponsor the study of classical antiquities and to finance their publication; three volumes of the *Antiquities of Athens* were brought out in 1762, 1788, and 1790, and three more on *Ionian Antiquities* in 1769, 1797, and 1840, containing the work of (among others) Stuart and Revett, Chandler, and Gell. Gell's Ionian expedition in 1812 paused on its way to Smyrna to excavate at Eleusis, and on the return journey to excavate and measure the Temple of Nemesis at Rhamnous, and to examine the Sunium and Thorikos area, with results published in 1817 as *The Unedited Antiquities of Attica*. In 1846 Francis Penrose lectured before the Society on Athenian Architecture; thereafter the Society sponsored his work on the Acropolis and its publication, in 1852, as *Investigation of Athenian Architecture* and, four years later, his *Principles of Athenian Architecture*. He became a member of the Society in 1852, and survived to become its 'Father'.

The Society's historians, Lionel Cust and Sydney Colvin, (*History of the Society of the Dilettanti* (London Macmillan) 1898), record a serious falling off, from about 1830 to 1880, in support and enthusiasm for classical antiquities: 'The Dilettanti and the British Museum were the only two institutions which practically kept the study alive in this country . . . A wave of Gothic enthusiasm had succeeded the preceding wave of classical enthusiasm among the most cultivated circles in England . . . Again, among persons really interested in antiquarian exploration, the brilliant discoveries of Sir Henry Layard and his coadjutors on the sites of the ancient Assyrian civilisation served for a while to divert attention from Greece and Rome'. They contrast these phenomena with the flourishing state of archaeology and art history at German universities: 'While every German University of note had its active and often brilliant school of classical archaeology, the subject was to all intents and purposes ignored in the curriculum and the class-lists of Oxford and Cambridge'. Only the work of Charles Newton, for the British Museum, at the great sites in Asia Minor brought fresh splendour to classical archaeology.

Not all British scholars, however, were indifferent to antiquities, and not only scholars were stirred by the discoveries of the German excavators at Olympia and by Schliemann's startling finds at Troy and Mycenae. Two of these were ancestral to the School, one directly, (Sir) Richard Jebb, then Professor of Greek at Glasgow, later Regius Professor of Greek at Cambridge, the other vicariously. This was Professor Mahaffy of Dublin, who in 1877 introduced to Greece for an extended tour the young George Macmillan who, though a King's Scholar at Eton, was destined by his father for a career in the family publishing firm. After his return to London George wrote to all Macmillan's classical clients to propose the formation of a Society for the Promotion of Hellenic Studies. The response was favourable — though one correspondent substituted 'Prevention' for 'Promotion' — and the Society came into being in 1879, with George as its first Honorary Secretary. Among its first stated objects were 'the assistance and guidance of English Travellers in Greece, and the encouragement of exploration and excavation in Greek lands'. It may be noted that the Archaeological Institute of America, founded in the same year on the impetus of Charles Eliot Norton, had as its first item of business 'the establishment of an American School in Athens'.

Jebb, also active in promoting the Hellenic Society, had been impressed on a visit to Athens in 1878 with the extent to which England lagged behind France and Germany in the study of ancient life and art, and its bearing on classical scholarship. In letters to the *Times* and the *Contemporary Review* he drew attention to this, and set out schemes for British Schools at Athens and at Rome. Returning to Greece in 1881 he discussed with the authorities of the École Française the possibility of admitting British students as members, but the Council of the Hellenic Society feared that such an arrangement might be prejudicial to the establishment of a British School in Athens, and nothing came of it. Jebb then entered into an extensive correspondence with possible supporters of such a school — including the Greek Foreign Minister, M. Kharilaos Trikoupis, who was enthusiastically in favour — and in May 1883 sought the publicity of an article in the *Fortnightly Review* (whose editor was the sympathetic T. H. Sweet-Escott) with 'A plea for a British Institute in Athens'.

An immediate response to this was the initiative taken by the Price of Wales; within a few weeks, on 25th June, he summoned a meeting at Marlborough House to discuss the establishment of such a school. The Meeting, which was attended by many distinguished figures, including Mr. Gladstone, Lord Salisbury and Lord Rosebery, resolved unanimously that the time had indeed come for this, and a strong committee was formed to carry out the scheme. It was clear from the outset that there would be no help from government funds, but more than £4,000 was promised in donations; an executive committee then came into being 'with the task of building the house in Athens and of appealing to learned bodies and to individuals for the funds necessary to the maintenance of the school'. To this committee Jebb and Sweet-Escott acted as Honorary Secretaries, assisted by Macmillan and Walter Leaf, who also acted as Honorary Treasurer.

The Greek Government's approval was sought and granted, and the Official Gazette for June 3, 1884 records the generous gift of a site on the lower slopes of Lykabettus (see Appendix I). A surprising omission from this definition of the School's boundaries is any mention of a road to its north, but this, Odos Spevsippou, must have been in existence by 1887, when the American School's new building was completed on the adjacent site, and was presumably necessary earlier

The School (now the Director's house), by F. C. Penrose in 1886

Francis Penrose,
the first Director, 1886–7

during the construction of the British School itself. The site was still outside the town; for many years visitors complained of its distance from the centre, and the planners of the American School nearly rejected their site as being half-an-hour from the shops and over a mile from the Acropolis.

For the British School's building the higher, northern end of the site was selected. It was designed by Penrose, who later became its first resident as Director. His drawing of it decorates the cover of the first volume of *BSA*; it shows a rectangular stuccoed house of two storeys, lying roughly east-west, with marble steps at the eastern approach and a pillared verandah on both floors looking south to Hymettus. In the drawing it stands on a terrace — which survives — with as yet no garden and few trees near it, and behind it rises the steep bare slope of Lycabettus, not yet planted with trees. Within, the house provided living quarters for the Director (as it still does), with some extra rooms where students might be accommodated, and a large upstairs room for the Library and for lectures. It was lighted by oil lamps, heated by coal fires, and devised for bedroom ablutions in hip baths. A large cistern to its east helped to secure the water-supply through the long dry summers.

The School's year has always begun in the autumn, and it was in November 1886 that Penrose came into residence as the first Director. The first student arrived in

Ernest Gardner,
Student 1886–7,
Director 1887–95

December; this was Ernest Gardner of Gonville and Caius College, Cambridge, Craven Student; the second, the Oxford Craven Fellow David Hogarth, followed early in 1887. Both men went on to become Directors, Gardner as immediate successor to Penrose in 1887. Little else is recorded about this interesting period since the first volume of the Minutes of the Managing Committee, from 1895 onwards the source of so much material for the School's history, has been lost for many years.

From 1887 the activities of the School assume a more familiar pattern. Five new students were admitted, two of them Royal Academy Travelling Students: R. Weir-Schultz and S. Barnsley, the first in a distinguished line of students of Byzantine art and architecture. The School's main field of work was Cyprus (since 1878 administered by Britain, though still Turkish teritory), for which an excavation fund had been set up by the Hellenic Society, with contributions from the School Committee and the Universities of Oxford and Cambridge. The Dilettanti's funds were tied up in the production of a new edition of Penrose's book on Athenian architecture and in supporting his investigations of the Hekatompedon, so they were unable to contribute. Director and students dug at

David Hogarth,
Student 1886–7,
Director 1897–1900

Old Paphos, at the site of the Aphrodite temple, at Salamis, and at Polis tes Chrysochou, the supposed site of ancient Arsinoe. Their reports were published with admirable promptitude in the *Journal of Hellenic Studies* (hereafter *JHS*), in which also the annual report on Archaeology in Greece, previously contributed by Jane Harrison, was now, as for the future, written by the School Director. From 1891 the School was also digging at Megalopolis. No less than eleven students were admitted in 1889, not all of whom, however, were engaged in these excavations. One was J. G. Frazer, collecting material for his magisterial commentary on Pausanias.

An important event of 1891 was the first visit to Greece of W. Flinders Petrie, whose recent excavations at Kahun and Gurob had recovered pottery which he recognised as Aegean. During his stay with the Gardners, he was able to see not only the great Bronze Age sites of the Argolid but also the material from Schliemann's and Tsountas' excavations. From his study of these, and their comparisons with his Egyptian material, he was able to advance the first proper estimate of Aegean relationships with Egypt, and to propose a firm date for the Mycenae tombs between the fourteenth and twelfth centuries B.C. Commenting,

Gardner remarked that Petrie 'had done more in a week than the Germans had done in ten years to clear up the matter'. In the following year Petrie dug at el Amarna, and found the considerable quantity of Mycenaean pottery which has ever since been the linchpin of Aegean Bronze Age dating.

In 1890 the first woman student was admitted, Eugenie Sellars, later, as Mrs. Strong, to become a leading authority on Roman art and archaeology. The library received an important accession of books thanks to the generosity of Sir Charles Newton, who handed over to the School more than £400, a substantial part of the fund raised on his retirement from the British Museum in recognition of his eminent services to classical archaeology. Over the next four years the School had plenty of good students — R. Carr Bosanquet, a future director, was admitted first in 1892 — but little money. Minor and not very productive short campaigns were undertaken at Abae in Phokis and at Aegosthena (with results published in the *JHS* 15 (1895) by E. F. Benson, the future novelist), but by 1894 the School's always precarious finances did not allow any digging in Greece. John Myres did some work in Cyprus, where he also compiled a catalogue of the Nicosia Museum, and two students assisted in experimental excavations at Alexandria conducted by Hogarth for the Egypt Exploration Fund.

The new lease of life which came to the School in 1895 has been described with evident heart-felt satisfaction by George Macmillan (*BSA* 17 (1910) xii): 'More than once the idea of an appeal for Government support had been mooted privately, but had met with no encouragement. The School, however, had an invaluable friend in Mr. (now Sir) Edwin Egerton, the British Minister at Athens, and it was largely at his instance that the Committee at last decided to make an appeal to the Treasury. Mr. Egerton had paved the way by drawing up and circulating early in 1894 a memorandum contrasting the meagre revenues of the British School with the far ampler funds at the disposal of the French, German and American Schools . . . Early in 1895 an appeal to the Treasury was drawn up and was signed not only by a large number of private individuals prominent in Church and State and in various departments of public life, but also by the official representatives of the British Museum, the National Gallery, the Royal Academy, the Royal Society, the Royal Institute of British Architects, the Society of Antiquaries, the Society of Dilettanti, the Hellenic Society, the Universities of Oxford, Cambridge, Dublin, St. Andrews, Glasgow, Aberdeen, Edinburgh, Durham, the Victoria University and other provincial Universities, King's College and University College, London, and all the leading public schools. This document . . . suggested that an annual grant of £500 a year would be amply justified. It was presented in June to Lord Rosebery as First Lord of the Treasury and Sir William Harcourt as Chancellor of the Exchequer. Within a few days the Ministry resigned . . . but happily before leaving office Sir William Harcourt had recorded a minute in favour of the grant of £500 being made for a period of five years, and his successor, Sir Michael Hicks-Beach, in due course confirmed the grant'.

'But this most welcome addition to its funds did not exhaust the good fortune of

Cecil Harcourt Smith,
Director 1895–7

the School, in this its *annus mirabilis* . . . Mr. Egerton had been working for its benefit in another direction, and had succeeded in persuading H. R. H. the Prince of Wales . . . to summon another meeting with the object of improving its financial position. This meeting, over which the Prince again presided, was held at St. James's Palace on July 9th, 1895, and attended by a large and distinguished company . . . The meeting yielded fresh annual subscriptions to the amount of £300 . . . and donations to the amount of £800 . . . It will be seen at once that the school had now entered upon a new and happier era'.

Ernest Gardner, having seen the School through so many difficult years, resigned to become Yates Professor of Classical Archaeology at University College London. The next Director, Cecil Harcourt Smith, came from the Greek and Roman Department of the British Museum, having been given two years' leave of absence by the Trustees for this purpose, not without considerable reluctance. His training in administration and his clear vision of the possible and the desirable played no small part, now that means were available, in shaping the School's future. The first *desideratum* was the enlargement of its premises by the erection of a residential hostel; the second was the founding of the *Annual*. The third, less concrete, which time to come could alone bring to fruition, was a scheme to coordinate the work of the foreign schools in Athens, first by a common policy in library provision, and secondly by each choosing some field in which its students might make a joint contribution to knowledge without interference with their own chosen work. Cordial approval of the policy of coordination was given by the heads of the French School and the German Institute.

The Managing Committee had for some time felt the desirability of a residence for students. 'Hitherto', reads the *Annual Report* for 1895/6, 'the students have found accommodation in various hotels or private lodgings in Athens, necessarily at a considerable distance from the School. The disadvantage to students of living so far from the library and from the natural centre of the School work is obvious . . . the advantage would be great of having the members collected close at hand, and living a common life under one roof. Real cooperation in work, and the mutual intercourse which is so valuable a feature in academic life at home, could thus be far better secured than is now possible'. The Hostel now to be erected, for which a special appeal for funds was made, was to contain accommodation for at least nine students, with common rooms, and quarters for staff. The site chosen was at the lower end of the *temenos*; the first sod was cut on the first day of January, 1895, and the foundation stone laid by the Queen of the Hellenes within the month. The plans, with which Penrose gave some help, were drawn up by the School Architect, Charles Clark; their execution was closely followed by both architect and Director — 'Mr. Clark and myself . . . may claim to have personally superintended the

The Hostel, east side, 1937

placing, I may almost say, of every stone' (*BSA* 3 (1897) 231) — or, during their absence at the excavations in Melos, by the Royal Academy Travelling Student, Pieter Rodeck, a nephew of Alma Tadema. Their building forms the core of the present Hostel. Built, with a façade of polygonal stonework, on two floors over a service basement, this very considerable house was completed in about seven months, at the very moderate cost of £1,500. The axis was oblique to the boundaries so that the view from the Common Room and its terrace (completed later) could focus on the Parthenon. Part of the roof was flat, 'commanding superb views of the Saronic Gulf and the valley to Pentelicus' — *o si sic semper!* By the end of the year the students were in residence. Its title, the Macmillan Hostel, commemorates the retirement of George Macmillan as Honorary Secretary, a post to which, however, he returned for a time a few years later while his successor, William Loring, was serving in the Boer War.

From 1886 to 1895 work done at the School was published in the *Journal of Hellenic Studies*; the School's subscribers received only the Annual Reports and the Proceedings of the Annual Meeting. With the School's financial position more securely established, it was felt that its work should be put on record in its own publication and the first *BSA* was brought out in 1895.

Harcourt Smith's report, after his first year in office, provides both a glimpse of life at the School in 1896 and a vision of its enlargement: 'What is not generally remembered . . . is that in Athens we have all the elements to hand of the finest and most varied archaeological teaching which Europe can produce . . . Any student of any school could have attended, if he chose, all the following courses of lectures: on the topography and monuments of Athens, on archaic art, history, sculpture, epigraphy in its philological aspect, Attic inscriptions, vases, and early Christian archaeology; all these given by trained scholars, some by acknowledged masters of their subjects. Besides this, almost every week has at least one or more meetings for the discussion of archaeological questions, either at one of the Schools or at the Greek archaeological societies, to which all students are invited . . . I hope it will not be considered Quixotic if I say that I look forward to a day when there may be something approaching to an international archaeological university in Athens'.

Melos was selected as the venue for the School's next excavation, and after survey and various trials elsewhere in the island the site of Phylakopi was chosen. As a preliminary, a small excavation was conducted in Athens in the spring at Kynosarges, where an early Greek gymnasium and a number of tombs were discovered. The Bronze Age towns of Phylakopi, the first such site to be explored in the Cyclades, occupied the School for three years, and its publication, brought out in 1904, is still of great importance for Aegean studies.

Harcourt Smith duly returned to the British Museum in 1897, where, in 1904, he became Keeper of the Greek and Roman Department. In 1909 he moved to the Victoria and Albert Museum — when he was knighted — where he remained until 1924. Thereafter he was for twelve years first Adviser, then Surveyor, of the Royal Collections of works of Art. Meanwhile, the long-delayed liberation of Crete from

Turkish rule opened up the island to archaeological work; in 1899 a Cretan Exploration Fund was formed, under the joint administration of Arthur Evans and the School, where Hogarth had in 1897 succeeded Harcourt Smith. The *BSA* for the following year carried the first of Evans' reports from Knossos; Hogarth was also digging in the Knossos area, Minoan houses on Gypsades and Roman tombs. He also explored the Dictaean Cave at Psychro, and, in the following year, the 'pits' and some large Minoan houses at Kato Zakro; his work was troubled by unprecedented floods in the Zakro plain, and he missed the Minoan palace, which remained undisturbed for another sixty years. After leaving the School he went on to dig at Naucratis and later at Ephesus; later still he succeeded Sir Arthur Evans as Keeper of the Ashmolean Museum in Oxford. Bosanquet, who succeeded to the Directorship in 1900, continued work on Cretan sites, first at Praisos, high in the hills of Siteia, and then for six years at the Minoan seaside town of Palaikastro.

Melos, the site of Phylakopi (photo, Colin Renfrew)

R. Carr Bosanquet,
Director 1900–06

   Robert Carr Bosanquet was Director for six years, having spent five years in
Athens as student and one as Assistant Director. From a letter to his sister Caroline
(preserved in *Letters and Light Verse*, edited by Ellen S. Bosanquet, 1938) can be seen
the changes in the School's appearance since Penrose's day: 'Turn to the right over
50 yards of villainous road and get out at a gateway with a plain wooden gate, and
a high stone wall above which olive trees show their silver-white branches. This is
the short cut into our temenos or paddock. The real carriage entrance is above,
with iron gates. Once inside the paddock, which is common to us and the American
School, you behold 3 houses. Just before you, approached by a steep uphill road, is
the students' hostel, a plain and obviously new building. On the right in the
background is the American School, 3 stories high and somewhat irregular, with a
fine marble balcony, a stretch of flat roof and a noble poplar . . . And on the left of
the background, half hidden by the Hostel from anyone entering the lower gate, is

the British School, a low two-storey building, well-proportioned with its long white verandah in front and its garden growing up luxuriantly all about it. You walk up the roadway past the Hostel, up a path to a flight of marble steps that connects the School garden with the paddock. The paddock by the way has still enough olives to show that it used to be the olive grove of the monastery until the Government laid hands on it for our benefit. Up the marble steps, past one of the young palms of which we are proud, up two more marble steps, and you have the little School house white and clean on your left, the American School garden on your right, and the iron carriage gates leading into the public road straight before you. You mount more marble steps — you are in a marble country remember — and ring. A stern-faced butler . . . surveys you through the grated upper half of the door and admits you'.

The first decade of the century was a particularly memorable one for the School. Its excavations were extensive and of high standard; their quality and scientific approach has been praised both by Georg Karo and Carl Blegen. Many of its students, such as Marcus Tod, F. W. Hasluck, Richard Dawkins and Alan Wace, were able to spend several years in Greece, and thereby become scholars of distinction as well as experience. One student of this period, John Marshall, went on in 1902 to India, to the Archaeological Survey, of which he in time became, as Sir John, Director-General. Looking back in 1936 on the occasion of the Athens Jubilee, he wrote: 'It is not too much to say that whatever archaeological exploration has since achieved in India and Burma has been in a large measure due to the teachings of the British School at Athens . . . up to 1902, when I went to India, no scientific excavation of any kind had been essayed in India, nor was archaeology taught in any Indian University or other institution. It fell to me, therefore, to be its first exponent, and to train up a body of students whose work is still based on the traditions and methods developed on the soil of Greece'. Some part of this tradition is to be seen in the 'Suggested work and teaching' scheme, formulated by Bosanquet, which first appeared in *BSA* 6 (1900) and was repeated thereafter for many years (Appendix II). The School's importance in the life of Athens was assisted by the friendship between the Bosanquets and the Egertons, at the Legation, who extended their interest and hospitality to the other members of the School. Marcus Tod acted for a time as tutor to some of the Greek Royal Family. Bosanquet acted as Assessor for the Athens preliminaries to the 1906 Olympic Games, at which he was, with Lord Desborough, the British Representative.

There were great developments also in the library. For years the School had sought to secure the library left by the historian George Finlay; in 1900 his remaining executor, W. H. Cooke, presented not only the books but even the shelves which housed them (as well as some antiquities), and so the large western common-room came to be the Finlay Library. The main library, still in the Upper House, was — not for the last time — outgrowing its shelf space. After the death of Penrose in February 1903, money was raised to build an extension to the north of

The Penrose Library and Hostel, west front, 1904, by Heaton Comyn

the Hostel, and named after him the Penrose Library. It was opened by Crown
Prince Constantine in April 1904. It comprised a transverse section, conforming
with the style, and extending to the full width and height, of the existing building;
this provided two studies (later bedrooms) on the upper floor; further to the north a
single-storey section, with clerestory windows, housed the main reading-room. The
architect was Heaton Comyn, a student of the School, from whose report to the
Royal Institute of British Architects, a copy, of which is lodged in the School,
several of our illustrations are taken. Marcus Tod, Assistant Director and
Librarian, was responsible for relocating the books, and cards in his exquisite
handwriting survived in the catalogue until after the second war.

Though the excavations in Crete continued until 1906, the focus of the School's
work began in 1904 to shift towards Laconia. At Bosanquet's instigation, Tod and
Wace began to compile a catalogue of the Sparta Museum, and an extensive survey
by several students of Laconian sites and topography was organised; small
excavations were conducted at Angelona, Geraki, and Koutiphari (Thalamai). A
Laconian Excavation Fund was opened to subscriptions in London, and enough
money was collected for digging to begin at Sparta in 1906.

The festivities of 1905 and 1906 perhaps demand special record. In 1905 Athens
was the scene of an Archaeological Congress, presided over by the Crown Prince.
The School gave a garden party for the Congress, at which a Greek Military Band

played. Queen Alexandra visited the School, together with the King and Queen of Greece and several Danish princes. In April/May 1906 the Olympic Games were celebrated in Athens; British athletes were entertained at the School and two of the team for the Marathon race were put up in the Hostel. King Edward — the School's Patron since his accession — was in Athens with Queen Alexandra, Princess Victoria, and the Prince and Princess of Wales, then on their way home from India. The Director took the King round the Acropolis before he, and Mrs. Bosanquet, at four hours' notice, gave a tea-party for the British royal visitors, the King and Queen of Greece, the Crown Prince and Princess, Prince George of Crete, Prince and Princess Nicholas, Prince Andrew, Prince Christopher, their suites and members of HBM Legation.

In 1906 Bosanquet retired to take up the newly founded chair of Classical Archaeology at Liverpool University. He was succeeded by Richard MacGillivray Dawkins, who had been at the School since 1902, and for two years in charge of the work at Palaikastro. By training an engineer and by choice a student of language and dialect, he was also an excellent excavator. His deep interest in customs and

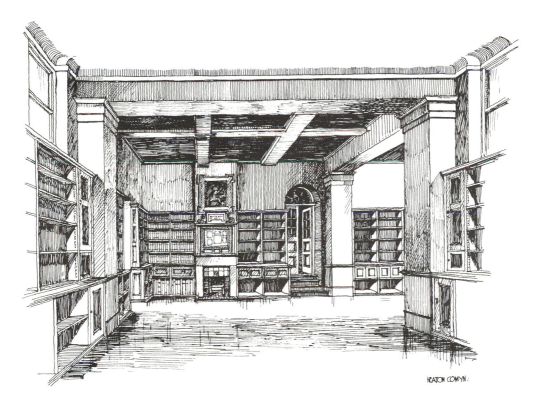

The Penrose Library, east end, 1904, by Heaton Comyn

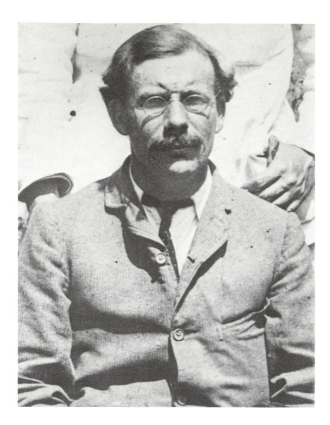

Richard Dawkins,
Director 1906–14

folklore he shared with F. W. Hasluck, student since 1901, Librarian in 1905–6, who now became Assistant Director; together they travelled extensively in the islands and in Anatolia, where Dawkins laid the foundations of his remarkable collection of Greek embroideries as well as his unrivalled knowledge of Modern Greek language and folklore.

The School's main effort was now directed to excavating the site of Artemis Orthia at Sparta with results which revolutionised all previous ideas about the artistic achievements of archaic Sparta. The Sparta Museum Catalogue was completed and published in March; the Greek authorities showed their satisfaction by inviting the School to undertake a catalogue of the Acropolis Museum. Other excavations were inaugurated in this session; the first of many campaigns in the cemetery at Rhitsona in Boeotia was begun by Professor Burrows, of Cardiff, and continued by Professor and Mrs. Percy Ure. 'For the first time in the history of Boeotian grave-digging every vase from every grave opened has been preserved, and the full contents of each grave kept carefully separate' (*BSA* 14 (1908)). At Theotokou in Thessaly Wace began work on the series of sites, mainly prehistoric, explored and published with Maurice Thompson (*Prehistoric Thessaly* 1912). By the

F. W. Hasluck,
Assistant Director
1911–15

end of 1907 the Laconian Excavation Fund was exhausted, but a generous gift of £1,000 from W. W. Astor allowed the work on the Orthia site to be continued, and exploration to be extended to the Menelaion on the hills east of the Eurotas. It was hoped that a Mycenaean palace might lie beneath the classical shrine of Menelaos and Helen; the finds were indeed Mycenaean, but of not very impressive houses. Before work in Laconia was concluded, in 1909, the Eleusinion site at Kalyvia tes Sochas, in the Taygetos foothills, was briefly investigated.

The Sparta dig had been expensive and its results copious. The session of 1909–10 was largely devoted to bringing up to date the arrears of publication of Palaikastro and Sparta, both of which however were many more years in gestation, largely owing to the 1914–18 war. Bosanquet and Ormerod spent some time in the new Heraklion Museum (begun 1907) arranging the finds from British excavations. Work continued however at Rhitsona, and in Thessaly was extended to Tsani, Lianokladi and Tsangli. The following session saw a short but valuable return for two months digging at Phylakopi.

Schemes for excavating Greek sites in Turkey had often to be considered; offers to contribute largely to digging expenses were made in respect of Cyzicus (in 1901) and Xanthos or another site in Lycia (also 1901), and a *firman* to dig at Colophon was offered and seriously considered, but none of these came to anything. A firm project for work at Datcha (Knidos), mooted in 1910, had to be abandoned when the outbreak of the First Balkan War in 1912 put Turkey in a state of war.

In 1911 the School celebrated it 25th birthday with a spate of publications and a dinner in London for about 130, in the Whitehall Rooms of the Hotel Metropole. Macmillan's History of the School appeared in *BSA* 17, followed by a bibliography (compiled by John Baker-Penoyre) of students' work other than that appearing in *BSA*; Arthur Woodward completed an Index of the first sixteen volumes of *BSA*, and Volume I of the Acropolis Museum Catalogue by Guy Dickins was published by the Cambridge University Press. There was also an exhibition of drawings. Congratulatory telegrams were sent by King George of the Hellenes, Professor J. R. Wheeler (Columbia) in the name of the American School, and from Hasluck, Thompson and Wace in Athens on behalf of the staff and students.

During the next two years the School returned to Crete to dig, first at the Kamares Cave, and then in Lasithi at Plati, where large Late Minoan buildings were uncovered. Though Greece was at war, members of the School were active in all areas; the report for 1912 makes special mention of Arnold Toynbee, whose 'record for travel is a remarkable one', being affected neither by season nor difficulties, the latter including, on one occasion, his arrest. In *Experiences*, published in 1969, he recalls that he covered between two and three thousand miles on foot in his nine months' stay. It is pleasant to read his impressions of other members of the School, notably Hasluck, Wace and Thompson, who 'made it their business to be helpful to a newly arrived junior student'. When they could they were as energetic in travel as he; Wace and Thompson 'indifferent to heat, hunger, cold or exposure to the elements . . . travelled like klephts, with the minimum of impedimenta'. In Athens, nurses working in a temporary hospital at the Marasleion were given quarters in the Hostel, and students got up a subscription to the Greek Red Cross. Thanks to the good offices of Sir Francis Elliot, the British Minister to Greece, the billeting of soldiers at the School was averted.

With Macedonia now united to Greece, Olynthus was discussed as a possible site for excavation, but the outbreak of the Great War made such a prospect, though not instantly abandoned, increasingly remote. At the the beginning of the 1914 session Dawkins had resigned and Wace, the new Director, and Hasluck, still Assistant, were both in England; they returned as soon as they could and in December reported the School to be 'in full working order'.

Alan Wace,
Director 1914–23

Alan John Bayard Wace first entered the School in 1920 to study Hellenistic Art; this was also his subject as Librarian of the School at Rome. On his first visit to Thessaly, however, he 'fell in love' with Neolithic pottery, and from that time prehistory became pre-eminently his field. Like Dawkins and Hasluck he also made serious studies of the contemporary life of Greece, and in particular of the embroideries and textiles, which fitted him for a second career, during the years when excavation in Greece was barred to him, as Keeper of Textiles in the Victoria and Albert Museum for the ten years from 1924.

Whether there were still any students in Greece at that time is not recorded, but 'in issuing their report for the session 1914–15 the Managing Committee beg to state that it has been . . . neither possible nor reconcilable with public opinion to do more than give facilities to such few students, and ex-students, as are ineligible for the National Service, and to maintain the School in good working order' (*BSA* 21 (1914–1916) 185). Gordon Childe was admitted as an Associate, but it is not clear whether he ever went to Athens at this time. Hasluck resigned as Librarian and Assistant Director, and both he and his wife were absorbed into British Government agencies. The Director, on his return, was seconded to the Legation and became Director of Relief for British Refugees from Turkey. The lack of students made possible the reorganisation of the Library and the fuller cataloguing of the Finlay books (by Hasluck) and papers (by Wace). Wace found relaxation in cherishing the garden and working on Mycenae pottery in the National Museum; later in the war he undertook, with Myres, the reorganisation of the School collection of antiquities.

Compton Mackenzie (*First Athenian Memories* (1931), *Greek Memories* (1939), *Aegean Memories* (1940)) was lodged, with other British officials, for some months of 1915 in the Hostel, and there compiled, with Hasluck, the counter-espionage catalogue of suspect persons. He was a frequent guest at lunch in the Upper House, and writes warmly of the Director as 'a delightful combination of great scholarship and humour'. It was an enquiry of Mackenzie's which led Wace to evolve that system of Passport Control (primarily to prevent undesirable travellers to Egypt) which 'was destined to serve as the model for passport bureaux all over the world' and kept him heavily employed for the rest of the war. (A naval visitor to the Hostel, Commander Potts, nearly broke his fist when, in the darkness of the entrance hall, he mistook a Roman bust for a lurking adversary, and punched it on the jaw when it refused to answer his challenge.)

In the political tensions of the unhappy winter of 1916–17 the Legation and all its functions transferred for three months to the Transport *Abbasieh*, moored off Keratsini, and B. H. Hill, Director of the American School, took charge of the British School buildings. After the Legation and the Director were able to return to Athens, the Hostel was opened to British subjects on Government work and was reported, in *BSA* 22 (1916–18), as very full.

Past members of the School were naturally enough serving in various capacities in and around Greece, four in Naval Intelligence and at least thirteen on the Salonica front, including Hilda Lorimer working in a Scottish Hospital there. Conspicuous among these was J. L. (later Sir John) Myres, 'Blackbeard of the Aegean', who was sent out by the Admiralty with the Dodecanese as his sphere of activity. With the tug *Syra* and armed bands raised *ad hoc* he raided the Anatolian seaboard (embarrassing the local Greek inhabitants by carrying off their cattle), thereby helping to tie down Turkish troops which might otherwise have been used against Allied forces elsewhere. In 1917 he became head of British Intelligence in Athens, and ended the war as Commander (temp) O.B.E. with the Greek Order of George Ist (see his son's amusing *10th Myres Memorial Lecture*, Leopard's Head Press, 1980). Dawkins, after a period in censorship and the Legation, was commissioned Lt. R.N.V.R and moved to Eastern Crete as Intelligence Officer (the question whether Naval Regulations would allow him to keep his moustache held up his commission for a while).

Marcus Tod was at Salonica, reading the Greek press and making translations of anything that might affect the Allied armies. In 1916, as Captain (Intelligence) he was transferred to the French sector and worked in censorship and the decoding of enemy ciphers. He was mentioned three times in despatches and was awarded the O.B.E. and the *Croix de Guerre avec palmes*. He also acted as compiler and editor of the ancient inscriptions noted in Macedonia in the course of their military duties by Stanley Casson, Ernest Gardner and Arthur Woodward, and saw to their publication in *BSA* 23 (1919).

On the other side of Greece Bosanquet was engaged with the Friends Ambulance Unit in relief work for the Serbs pushed back to the Albanian coast by the advancing Austrian army, and in their transfer to safety and rehabilitation in Corfu. Later he worked in Macedonia as director of the Serbian Relief Fund.

The departure of King Constantine and the Allied recognition of Venizelos as head of the legal Government of Greece simplified the British position in Athens but brought complications to the School. Because the Director was now employed full time by the Legation and the Hostel was in constant use as a hotel for persons on official or military business, the School's £500 annual grant from the Government was from June 1917 transferred to the Foreign Office Vote. The nature of this arrangement was in part misunderstood by Myres, who submitted a grandiose scheme for the School to become a centre for propaganda — in the widest sense — and the gradual assimilation of various spheres of Greek life to British ways. He coupled the scheme with criticism of the Director for not doing more to make use of the Hostel and for the comfort of its residents, especially Service personnel, as part of the general war effort. The Managing Committee was assured by the Foreign Office that it was not in favour of the Myres scheme, and specifically denied any intention to take over the School or its functions; the Foreign Office letter concluded with an expression of appreciation of the great services rendered by the School during the war. Myres was accordingly informed by the Committee that his proposals were 'incompatible with the objects for which the School was founded, and that under the circumstances any action in such a direction on their part would be *ultra vires* and could not be entertained'. Other suggestions, advanced by Wace, for widening the School's sphere of work, for example by the study of Greek geology or botany, were briefly considered after the war but, perhaps fortunately, came to nothing. The current much-enlarged scope of work done at the School would have delighted him. Hasluck, in the early years of the war a great mainstay of British Intelligence in Athens, succumbed in 1916 to the tuberculosis from which he had for some years suffered. With his wife he left Greece for a sanatorium in Switzerland, where he died on February 22nd 1920. Mrs. Hasluck in time settled in Albania, where she made herself the acknowledged expert on that country's customs and folklore.

The question of extending the School's property by the purchase, conjointly with the American School, of land lying north of Odos Spevsippou occupied the Director and the Managing Committee seriously during the years before and after the Armistice. (This topic is dealt with in Chapter II(b)).

The School returned to archaeology in the autumn of 1919. Wace was reappointed Director for a further three years and released, reluctantly, by the Legation from a valuable spell of work for refugees from Turkey. Stanley Casson became Assistant Director, though a third of his time was preempted by an archaeological Fellowship at New College, Oxford. Of the three new students two, Michael Tierney and Arnold Lawrence, were to become Professors. The Committee felt that 'the excavation of a classical site would be in the best interests of the School, as soon as this became possible', but acquiesced in the Director's suggestion, strongly supported by Sir Arthur Evans, of digging at Mycenae. Wace accordingly began his first campaign there in 1920; he was assisted by Arnold and Phyllis Gomme (old students), and Carl Blegen of the American School, at whose own wartime excavations at Korakou he had himself assisted. All the students spent some time at Mycenae; Casson was also excavating in Macedonia, at the iron-age site of Chauchitsa.

An outline scheme for widening the School's sphere of work was prepared, but foundered on the usual reef of inadequate finance. Subscriptions had naturally fallen off during the war, and a well-reasoned case presented to the Treasury for doubling the annual grant was refused (responsibility for the grant was resumed by the Treasury with effect from 1921). Another appeal for funds was circulated, and brought in £400 for Mycenae, but the latest BSA (vol.23) was the most expensive ever printed; another expense was the publication of the second volume of the Acropolis Museum Catalogue, edited before his death by Dickins and subsequently completed by Casson.

An important innovation in the winter of 1920 was the admission of women as residents in the Hostel. The political turmoil in Athens attendant on the rejection of Venizelos at the polls and the return of King Constantine prompted the Minister, Lord Granville, to press for this step in the interests of safety; it was a particularly apt moment, in that not only were there three women students, but two of the men, Bernard Ashmole and J. J. E. Hondius, were married, and so had to live out; the School was almost empty. To two of these women the School's historian is particularly indebted; to Winifred Lamb, access to many of whose letters has been generously given by her family; and Lilian Chandler (Mrs. Batey), the first holder of the Sachs Studentship, whose diary, given to the School by her sister, provides a fresh and lively picture of multifarious activities. From both these sources we learn how much the life of the School was enriched by the presence of F. B. Welch (a former student, then Vice-Consul attached to the Passport Control Office) who was engaged in work on the Finlay Papers, and how much good-fellowship and plain fun was engendered in the School by the ingathering. In 1921 Dutch, Norwegian, Swedish and Swiss students were admitted.

The Acropolis at Mycenae (photo, Sinclair Hood)

At Mycenae work began again in May 1921 and continued, with special funding, over the next two years. An enormous amount was achieved; *BSA* 24 (1921) and 25 (1921–23) carry reports of digging all over the acropolis hill, around and in the nine tholos tombs, with studies of the frescoes (by Winifred Lamb), of the Grave Circle sculptured stelai (by Walter Heurtley), and an account of Hellenistic Mycenae by Axel Boethius. In addition, the cemetery of Mycenaean Chamber Tombs on the Kalkani hill was cleared; at the invitation of the Society of Antiquaries (through Sir Arthur Evans) these were published as a complete number of *Archaeologia* (vol. 82). Because of disagreements with the dominant members of the Committee, Wace's tenure as Director was not renewed, and at the same time the promising excavations at Mycenae were abandoned until 1939.

The Committee was still anxious to work on a classical site, and it was decided to return to Sparta. Arthur Woodward, who succeeded Wace (after a year as Assistant Director) in 1923, had assisted at Artemis Orthia and was involved in its publication. The usual special appeal was issued for Sparta, and digging started in March 1924. The main area investigated was the theatre, but other parts of the acropolis were also explored; work continued until 1927. Casson, whose dig at

Arthur Woodward,
Director 1923–9

Chauchitsa was completed in 1922, took up a Lectureship in Oxford and was succeeded as Assistant Director by Heurtley, who began at once to dig in Macedonia, mainly in the Vardar valley. The Ures returned to work at Rhitsona, and in 1926/7 R. P. Austin (Reading University) excavated on a small scale at Haliartos, on the property of the Copais Company. (Published in *BSA* 27 (1925–6), 28 (1926–7)and 32 (1934).)

    The most notable event in the School's history during the 1920s was the generous gift by Sir Arthur Evans of all his property at Knossos, including the site of the Palace of Minos, the Villa Ariadne, and some adjacent land, mostly under vines. With the site he also made financial endowment to cover, with the rent from the vineyards, all expenses of upkeep. This munificent offer, promulgated in 1922, became fact in April 1926; Duncan Mackenzie, who had worked for many years as Evans' assistant, was appointed to the new position of Curator of Knossos, with responsibilities roughly similar to those of the Assistant Director in Athens, part of his salary again being guaranteed by Evans. The School thus for the first time acquired what the other foreign schools had long enjoyed, a permanent place of

George Macmillan,
first Honorary Secretary,
Chairman 1903–33

work outside Athens. The apparently inexhaustible site of Knossos has never ceased to provide work for British students of every period from Neolithic to Byzantine, and a focus for their studies comparable with Olympia or Samos for the Germans, Delphi, Delos or Mallia for the French, Corinth or the Athenian Agora for the Americans, or Phaistos for the Italians. Already in the session 1926–7 Forsdyke (later Sir John, Director of the British Museum) was digging Minoan tombs at Mavrospelio, to the east, and Humfry Payne Proto-geometric to fifth-century tombs to the north of the Palace of Minos.

Another act of constructive generosity was the Chairman's foundation in 1927 of the Macmillan Studentship, to be held at the School for two consecutive years. The Committee recorded with pleasure that it would 'provide a welcome revival of the type of 'long-period' student who did so much for the welfare of the School before 1914 — a type which has become all too scarce, owing to changed conditions, in the last 10 years'. The following year the donor visited Athens with his family, for the first time for several years, and gave 83 books (from the library of J. B. Bury) to the Library. The first to be appointed Macmillan Student was Humfry Payne, but he

Humfry Payne,
Director 1929–36

became Director shortly afterwards, and the first full-time holder was John Pendlebury. Since 1984 part of the Rodewald benefaction has been applied to this award, and it has been renamed the Macmillan/Rodewald Studentship.

While Heurtley continued to dig in Macedonia (A. Mamas and Molyvopyrgo) and Winifred Lamb (engagingly referred to in S. S. Hadjiannis' *History of Methymna* (1976) as Wini Fred Lamp) began work at Thermi in Lesbos, the Sparta dig came to an end, and Woodward resigned, to be succeeded in 1929 by Humfrey Payne, then only 27. His life and work has been so eloquently recorded by his wife, in *The Traveller's Journey is done* (1943) that this history can, and need, treat it lightly as only one aspect, though the most important one, of the life of the School during his directorship. Financially, it was one of the most straitened periods in the school's history; the Annual Report of November 1927 states 'the already slender funds of the School have dwindled by nearly £1,000 in three years'. Efforts to reduce the drain on funds by putting up Hostel rents led, in the early thirties, to student protests and an unwillingness to live in; the writer remembers being told of students living in Aegina to save up for periods in the Hostel. In 1932 the post of Assistant Director was (temporarily) abandoned to save money, the Macmillan Student,

Romilly Jenkins, being appointed Senior Student 'with the special duty of assisting the Director . . . the Director keeping in his own hands the administration of the Library'. At the same time the post of School Architect, held since 1924 by Piet de Jong, was left unfilled after his resignation. Heurtley moved to Jerusalem, where he became Librarian and Keeper of Archaeological Records in the Department of Antiquities of the Government of Palestine. His work in Macedonia, begun in 1924 at Vardino and continued over eight years, with assistance from many funds including the Macedonian Exploration Fund (placed at his disposal by the School Committee) was published by the Cambridge University Press in 1939 as *Prehistoric Macedonia*.

Payne, after a rather disappointing season at Eleutherna in Crete, started at Perachora, in 1930, the first of four immensely prolific seasons of excavation. He was assisted not only by some of the students (Robert Cook, Arthur Lane, Robert Hopper, André Kenny) but by James Brock (who had gained experience with Winifred Lamb at Antissa) and Gerard Young (who assumed the name of Gerard Mackworth-Young by deed-poll in 1947). In Young, Payne found the ideal collaborator for his next great undertaking, the study and publication of the *Archaic Marble Sculpture from the Acropolis* (1936).

Perachora, the site and harbour from the east, 1937

Thanks to the enthusiasm and exertions of Lord Rennell of Rodd, money was raised for 'Homeric' excavations in Ithaca, which began in 1931 at the site of Aetos, under the direction of Heurtley. These were followed by work at Pelikata (Heurtley) and the Polis cave (Sylvia Benton), where the proprietor of the land had some years before extracted parts of a bronze tripod-cauldron. Pelikata, though the obvious place for a palace of Odysseus, did not produce it, but from the cave came not only the famous sherd inscribed 'a vow to Odysseus', but pieces of twelve more tripods. Jenkins made two short trials at Isthmia, aimed at locating the site of the Temple of Poseidon. Winifred Lamb, her excavations at Thermi and Antissa in Lesbos completed, moved to Chios, where she conducted the first of what was to be a series of British digs in that island at the site of Kato Phana.

In Crete, John Pendlebury succeeded Mackenzie as Curator in 1929, dug, with Evans, in the Palace West Court, and started to work on his Guide and to organise and catalogue the Stratigraphical Collection. Payne too returned to Crete in 1935 to dig, with Alan Blakeway, the Geometric and later cemetery of Fortetsa. After the untimely deaths of both excavators the tombs were published *in extenso* by James Brock in 1954. The publication of Perachora also had to be achieved by others; the first volume, all but completed by Payne before he died, was finished and seen through the press by Tom Dunbabin; the second, in the preparation of which Dunbabin had the assistance of many who were students between 1936 and 1939, was on the point of completion before his own tragic death in 1955. It was finally brought out by Martin Robertson in 1962.

Payne's years as Director saw the arrival of several students who, apart from contributions in their own fields, were to serve the School well in later years: Romilly Jenkins, Martin Robertson, Nicholas Hammond and Robert Cook as Chairmen; John Cook and A. H. S. (Peter) Megaw as Directors; Tom Dunbabin as Deputy Director. With Payne in Athens and Beazley in Oxford (though paradoxically many of those concerned came from Cambridge!) it is not surprising that in those days vase-painting was a favourite field.

Excavations on Siphnos, recommended as a site by Payne even before he started at Perachora, were undertaken by Brock and Young, at the latter's expense, in 1934–5, and continued annually until 1938. Heurtley's move to Palestine, and Sylvia Benton's need to work on the Polis finds, brought a temporary interruption to digging in Ithaca, though Sylvia fitted in a small (Neolithic) dig at Astakos on the mainland of Akarnania, and another, with Hilda Lorimer, in Zakynthos.

1935 was the year of Italy's attack on Abyssinia and the consequent imposition of League of Nations sanctions against her. The British School at Rome admitted no students; it did not close, but its Director and Librarian travelled in Greece and the Levant; the School in Athens was enlivened by their visits and, for considerable periods, by the residence of several of the Rome students, including two sculptors. It was at about this time that admission to Student Privileges was instituted for short-stay or less qualified visitors.

1936 was a year of both sorrow and celebration. It was in May that Humfry

*Alan Blakeway,
Director 1936*

Payne died, very suddenly, of blood-poisoning, in the flower of his age and the full tide of his archaeological achievement. His friend and collaborator Alan Blakeway succeeded him as Director, but himself died before the year was out. A further loss to the School but not to archaeology was the appointment of Peter Megaw, on whose shoulders, as Acting Director after Payne's death, had fallen the whole Athens administration, to be Director of Antiquities in Cyprus. The celebration was of the School's Jubilee, with an exhibition at Burlington House (also shown in Manchester and Edinburgh) and a dinner at Princes Galleries attended by some ninety past and present friends and students. A Jubilee appeal for funds was also launched, and raised just under £2,000 in donations, new subscriptions, and Life Compositions.

Gerard Mackworth Young,
Director 1936–46

The new Director was Gerard Young. Coming late to Greek archaeology after retiring early from the Indian Civil Service, and considering himself too old to start research, he at first specialised in photography, collaborating with Payne not only on the beautifully produced book on the Acropolis marbles but in the excavations at Perachora and Knossos. In Athens, his initial impact was as administrator; to this was joined a personal generosity in refurbishing, largely at his own expense, both buildings then in a very run-down condition, and establishing the post of Athens Secretary which, in the capable person of Ruby Woodley, kept the Hostel and the library in good running order.

One happy result of the Jubilee increase in funds was the enlargement of the library. The Payne Room was added on the west, and at the north end a two-storey annexe was built for the museum and map-room above with a store-room below. The Museum provided space for the proper arrangement of the collections of photographs, antiquities and sherds.

In Crete, Pendlebury was replaced as Curator in 1935 by Richard ('Squire') Hutchinson, but continued to travel, and excavate sites in or above the Lasithi plain. Hutchinson was joined by a school party under Dunbabin for a small-scale excavation at Knossos in the spring of 1937, and partly dug a large Roman villa accidentally discovered just north of the Villa Ariadne. Two architectural students worked on the buildings of Chios, and Edith Eccles dug in the cave of Ayio Gala in that island. In 1937 Sylvia Benton resumed excavation in Ithaca at three sites in the north of the island, one of which, Tris Langadas, proved to be purely Mycenaean and occupied her for a second season. In 1938 she also spent several productive weeks at Aetos, where the rich temple deposit, partly cleared by Heurtley, was in danger from unauthorised digging. In the spring of 1938 the Director conducted a short excavation on the dump in front of the east end of the Acropolis, which recovered some missing pieces of known vases and part of an inscribed plaque.

The last year of peace saw the discovery (in December 1938) of the first canonical Late Minoan tholos tomb at Knossos, by Hutchinson, and Wace's successful return to Mycenae (in the Summer of 1939), which confirmed the existence of a prehistoric cemetery on the west slope of the acropolis outside the walls, shed a wealth of fresh light on the date and construction of the Treasury of Atreus, and recovered the most remarkable of all Mycenaean Ivories.

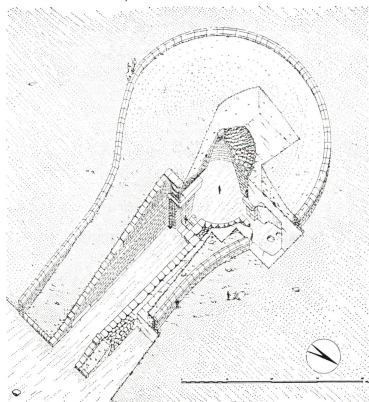

Mycenae,
isometric reconstruction
of the Treasury
of Atreus
(after Sinclair Hood)

When the war came, the school's posture was for some time debated. Might it not be better, like the Germans at Olympia, to continue with some of its work until the war effort should be more totally engaged? The Director was firmly opposed to the presence in Greece of male students of military age, maintaining — correctly, as the amazed Greek reaction to the young lecturers of the British Council showed — that Greek opinion would be unable to reconcile their presence with a positive view of Britain's military effort. He himself was engaged by the Legation as Director of Publicity (with David Wallace as Press Attaché), with his office in the Penrose Library and Miss Woodley combining her Press work with the oversight of the Hostel. Wace returned to his first-war job in Passport Control; such students as did not return to England found work in the Legation. The Hostel, as in the first war, accommodated persons on Government business including, this time, a large British Council contingent. A few students managed to work in the Library, and in March 1940 Wace addressed a large audience on Mycenae at an Open Meeting attended by the King of Greece. As the shadow of war drew nearer, he spent his spare moments in helping to pack up the contents of the National Museum.

At Knossos, the Curator dug a Late Minoan tomb near the Temple tomb and important Proto-geometric tombs at the Tekke, and found time to do some teaching of English for the British Council. In May 1940 he was joined by John Pendlebury, in name an extra Vice-Consul, in fact concerned with preparing Cretan resistance to an all too probable German or Italian attack.

In April 1941, with the German army five days away from Athens, the Director and the last residents of the Hostel left for Crete, spending about five days near Khania before going on to Egypt. The King of Greece stayed a few days at the Villa Ariadne before he too went on to Egypt, as did the Hutchinsons. Pendlebury, now in uniform, stayed until he was shot in the early days of the German invasion. During the evacuation of Greece in April 1941 Bernard Ashmole, serving in the RAF, was able to use his knowledge of Greek topography to secure the evacuation via Kalamata of hundreds of RAF groundstaff when the harbour at Nauplia was blocked by a burning wreck. In Athens the School buildings were left in charge of the Americans. When in December 1941 the United States became a belligerent they were handed over to the Swiss as Protecting Power; later the upper House was used as a relief distributing centre by the Swiss and Swedish Red Cross. Their life-saving work was commemorated by the renaming of the adjacent streets Alopekis and Spevsippou as Elvetias and Souedias respectively. The Villa Ariadne was occupied by the German General commanding in Crete; for the spectacular kidnapping of General Kreipe there in 1944 see chapter III(b). Meanwhile, in the hills of Crete, in Pindus, in the Peloponnese, old students, with various ranks and nick-names, were living as liaison officers with the guerillas, supplying arms and money, trying to compose their differences and to direct those arms against the Germans. Many served in the Forces, in all the theatres of war. Others, at their desks in London or in Cairo, were trying to apply their knowledge of Greece and its language to the greatest public good. (*BSA* 42 (1947) ix–xv).

The first British archaeologists to set foot in the School after the liberation of Greece in the autumn of 1944 were Robin and Mary Burn, then serving in the British Embassy. Robin's account is too vivid not to be quoted here: 'I was instructed to go to the School and make it ready to serve as an embassy mess. A Swiss diplomatic secretary was ready with the keys, and the Red Cross mission had already withdrawn, handing over its functions to the British Military administration, pending the further handover to the relief organisation UNRRA. Along with a soldier assigned to light duties . . . I got the beds out (they had been stacked in the library) and upstairs . . . The most remarkable thing was that the library tables, having had the Finlay books stacked on them for three years, had sagged and become hammock-shaped; but after the books had been taken off them they gradually, in not many weeks, resumed their original shape. In a corner of the library still lay piles of Gerard Young's news hand-outs. I looked to see how they ended . . . I read, dated April 17 1941, that the imperial forces were withdrawing from the Olympos line to new and stronger positions. So might have ended the archives of Boghaz Kôy'. The School and its inhabitants weathered the fighting of that unhappy winter unscathed. The Director, returning from war service in India, passed briefly through Athens in April of 1945 and returned in the autumn to assist in the task of rehabilitation and to define the school's sphere of action in the immediate future. The buildings remained in possession of the Embassy until, in October 1946, the school was able to resume its proper work and regained possession of the Upper House and the Penrose Library to do so.

Meanwhile at Knossos the Villa Ariadne was 'liberated', almost simultaneously, by Nikolaos Platon, by Tom Dunbabin, descending from his mountain fastnesses, and by Manoli Markoyiannakis, Evans' former houseboy. It was soon taken over for the Headquarters of the British Area Commander, whose business was largely the administration of relief supplies. The Taverna was handed over to UNRRA, which, thanks to some string-pulling by Dunbabin, came to be represented by Mercy Money-Coutts and Edith Eccles, both experienced Cretan archaeologists. By spring 1945 a beginning had been made in tidying up the Palace, both houses and the garden, and bringing the vineyards once more under cultivation. The old domestic staff, though two were frail and ripe for retirement, were back at the Villa. Manolaki (Akoumianakis) had been killed in action in May 1941, but his family continued to live at Knossos, and his elder son Michael was temporarily in care of the property. The Curator, released from G.H.Q. Cairo, was able to take over at Knossos late in 1945. He retired in 1947 and was succeeded by Piet de Jong.

The School's return to full-time archaeology in November 1946 was in every way a fresh start, since Young retired from the Directorship and Ruby Woodley too left Athens for England. At first it consisted of the new Director John Cook and his wife Enid (the first occupants of the Upper House since Bosanquet to have a young family) and a Librarian, whose most urgent task was to integrate into the library the noble collection of books selected by Dunbabin (after the Ashmolean Museum library in Oxford had had its pick) from those left by Sir Arthur Evans. In the

John Cook,
Director 1946–54

spring of 1947, after the last Embassy resident had left the Upper House, they were joined by a few students, old and new. Much of the countryside was still afflicted by guerilla warfare, travel was restricted, excavation on any scale (outside Athens, where the Americans were able to work in the Agora) was not permitted. Many of the major museums were still closed, awaiting the huge and expensive labour of reinstallation. In Crete, though the Heraklion Museum was shut, Dr. Giamalakis made his wonderful collection available to visitors, and Hutchinson, helped by Hilda Pendlebury, reconstituted the stratigraphic collection at Knossos. In Ithaca Sylvia Benton succeeded in rehabilitating the museum at Stavros.

Conditions in Greece remained difficult for several years — not least in the extremely steep rise in the cost of living — but in November 1947 the Hostel, relinquished by the Embassy during the summer, opened with a full complement of students and gave hospitality during the session to many 'wandering scholars', including, again, a party of Swedish archaeologists. (The new Swedish School was founded in May 1948 but was not yet able to house its members.) Excavation in Greece being still forbidden, the Director made a reconnaissance in Asia Minor, and in the summer embarked on a very fruitful joint excavation with a Turkish team, under Ekrem Akurgal, at the site of Old Smyrna at Bayrakli on the outskirts of the modern city. Work continued here, with the collaboration of James Brock and the help of many of the School students, until 1951.

By the spring of 1949, thanks in part to the 'Truman doctrine' and the extension of Marshall aid to Greece, the rebel movement had collapsed; the ban on excavation was lifted, and travel was possible all over the country, in conditions described (by John Cook) as quicker and more comfortable than before the war. The School in Athens and in Crete overflowed with students, and the buildings erected in the garden as storerooms by the Red Cross were re-roofed, plumbed, furnished, and fitted up as dormitories. At Knossos, where Palace, grounds and estate had been restored to order and productivity by the devoted work of Piet and Effie de Jong, tombs were dug, Minoan on the Ailias slope, Roman on the site of the new Heraklion sanatorium, by Piet and Sinclair Hood. In 1950 Wace was able to resume the work at Mycenae interrupted by the war, and to dig every summer, with great success, until 1955.

Viewed from London, the School's position became increasingly desperate over these post-war years. In spite of a Government grant large by pre-war standards and annually increasing, School finances were more precarious than ever; reporting in 1950 after the forced sale of £2,000 worth of securities to discharge some of the School's liabilities Mr Yorke said 'in the long period during which I have had the honour of being your treasurer (now more than 40 years) there has never been cause for so much anxiety with regard to our finances as at the present moment'. In such circumstances, and under pressure from Mortimer Wheeler, as Secretary of the British Academy (then contemplating the centralisation of the financing of all overseas archaeological institutions under its aegis), it was decided to offer to the Greek Archaeological Service the Palace of Minos, the Villa Ariadne,

Sinclair Hood,
Director 1954–62

and all the land at Knossos except the Taverna and a small enclave round it. The offer, made and gladly accepted in 1951, took effect in April 1952. The Taverna became a dig-house, and the next year a workroom was built and equipped beside it. The change of ownership made little difference to the tempo of excavation at Knossos, for which Sinclair Hood was mainly responsible.

Encouraged by an anonymous donation of £700 for the purpose, the School turned its attention to Chios. After a short excavation on the Kophina ridge, on the outskirts of Chios town, the main effort was directed to Emporio on the south coast, where three adjoining sites produced an Early Bronze Age settlement, an Archaic acropolis and town, and a Byzantine fort and basilica. The excavators (Hood on the Bronze Age site, John Boardman on the acropolis), whose teams included in

Emporio, Chios, the acropolis and harbour, 1954 (photo, John Boardman)

Sir John Myres,
Chairman and President, 1933–47

1955 a sizeable contingent of Swedish and Danish students, were joined for the 1954 season by an under-water team, 'The Sunday Times Expedition', directed by Richard Garnett with Dilys Powell as rapporteur. This was the first under-water exploration to be undertaken in Greek waters. Later the Sunday Times generously presented the aqualung to the School, and it was used the following year for a survey of Cretan harbours.

In 1954 John Cook retired from the Directorship to a readership (later a chair) at Bristol, and was succeeded in Athens by Sinclair Hood. Work in Chios did not prevent his continued explorations at Knossos, where Boardman too had dug some Proto-geometric tombs in 1953. The troubles in Cyprus, erupting in the last months of 1955, had serious repercussions on the School in Athens. Firebrand patriots threatened to attack the premises in January 1955, and, on Embassy advice, intending students were advised to postpone their arrival; no admissions to student privileges were permitted. Excavations were suspended, and an almost total boycott of the British School was observed by Greeks in official positions. By the end of the year, however, the situation in Greece was sufficiently calm for students to be once more admitted without restraint, and in summer 1957 excavation was resumed at Knossos on several sites, from the Neolithic of the Palace Central court to the Christian Basilica on the Sanatorium site. Another very important enterprise, the Knossos Survey, was approaching completion — it was published in November 1958 — and attracted a generous loan from the Council of Management of the Marc Fitch Fund, perhaps the first appearance in this rôle of one of the School's most notable benefactors. British work at Mycenae, interrupted by the Cyprus crisis and further suspended by the death of Wace in November 1957, was not resumed until 1959, when Lord William Taylour began work again on a joint programme with the Greek Archaeological Society.

It is not possible, in this skeleton survey, to note all the changes in personnel or to record the losses suffered increasingly with the passing years of old students and committee members. Exception must be made for the death of Myres, first and only President, in 1954: for the most untimely death in 1955 of Tom Dunbabin; of Wace,

Tom Dunbabin,
Deputy Director 1938–46

Vincent Yorke,
Honorary Treasurer 1906–57

still hoping to dig again at Mycenae, in 1957; of V. W. Yorke, Hon. Treasurer for more than 50 years, also in 1957. And the resignation in March 1962 of Edith Clay after 25 years as London Secretary, years in which 'Subscribers and Managing Committee alike leaned on her experience, knowledge and understanding of the School'.

The school's finances are dealt with in a separate chapter but they cannot be entirely ignored in an overall picture as their impact on the school's activities was often striking and felt not just by the administration but by the ordinary students. A government grant of more thousands than the pre-war hundreds, greatly increased subscriptions from colleges, universities and other bodies, and doubled subscriptions from ordinary subscribers, were still inadequate to keep in good order the now aging buildings in Athens, to house the ever growing number of books in the library, to pay proper salaries to Athens and London staff, and to meet the inflated cost of living. Students especially found their grants inadequate to keep them in Greece for a whole session; their numbers were seldom less than 20, but for months the School would be half empty. Pressure on shelf space made necessary enlargements to the Library which could only be met by appeals for public support

— generously responded to — and by the rather desperate measure of selling off part of the School's never large investments. Yet the desirable was achieved; in Athens, constant growth and organisation of its collections of maps, photographs and antiquities; the creation of an Assistant Director's flat over the Annexe(previously he lived in the Hostel), of new buildings against the western temenos wall to house storeroom and a pot-mender's workroom.

The largest accretion of all, the Stratigraphical Museum at Knossos, was made possible by two very generous subventions, of £2,500 from Dr. Joan Evans and of the outstanding balance of £2,240 from Marc Fitch. The purpose was to rehouse, close to the Villa Ariadne, the stratified material from Evans' excavations which remained stored, well-organised but in unsatisfactory conditions, in basements of the Palace, and, at the same time, to accommodate the steadily growing quantity of comparable material from current excavations. Work on the new building, started in the session 1960–61. Sinclair Hood, whose brainchild it was, retired from the directorship in 1962, but returned to Crete for a year as Honorary Curator of Knossos, to enable him to work on the finds from his many years' excavations.

Hood was replaced in Athens by Peter Megaw, who, since handing over the Cyprus Department of Antiquities to Porphyrios Dikaios, a former student of the School, had been working in Istanbul. His return to Athens after 25 years coincided with a welcome increase in the Government grant to £12,000. With 154 admissions, 36 of them full-time students, the School was once more full. Two seasons' work was done at the old site of Palaikastro by Hugh Sackett, Assistant Director since 1961, and Mervyn Popham, Macmillan Student; Lord William Taylour continued to dig in the Mycenae Citadel House, and a Cambridge team began work on an early Neolithic site at Nea Nikomedeia in Western Macedonia. In the summer of 1963 Nicolas Coldstream and George Huxley began work at Kastri in Kythera, on a Minoan site first recorded by Sylvia Benton, and Taylour led a team to Ayios Stephanos, a Bronze Age Laconian site noted by Richard Hope Simpson. With *Perachora* II finally in print, Jim Coulton began some preparatory clearing of the later parts of that site not included in the publication.

During the 1960s there were important developments in the Library. In 1960 Peter Fraser went out to Athens from All Souls College, Oxford, at the Committee's request, to make recommendations for filling *lacunae* and generally for the more efficient running and arrangement of the library. *Lacunae* were numerous; for some years book purchase had been financed by admission fees — hence perhaps an over-generous admissions policy which led to the overcrowding noted in the early 1960s. Filling the gaps proved an extensive, and expensive, operation but with time both books and money were found. The Cambridge Faculty of Classics gave a welcome £2,000 for the purchase of non-archaeological books (which it was hoped would encourage classical scholars of other specialities to spend time at the School).

Space was now the problem, for readers as well as books, and plans for an extension were prepared and an appeal launched to finance it. The response was generous (£5,588 recorded to July 1966); work began in July 1965 and the extension was completed and shelved within the year. This addition was located north of the Payne Room and west of the periodicals basement and the Museum/Map Room above it (opening off the north end of the Penrose Library). It provided a reading room with shelving for the Byzantine and later sections above an additional periodicals basement, and, beyond these, a typing room, a dark room and a new Museum. The basement under these last remained open as a carport pending further growth of the library. The most westerly section containing the library was aligned with the annexes built along the temenos wall in order to link them visually, if not structurally, with the main building. The plans were prepared by Evangelos Vasiliades working in close touch with the Director (at one time School Architect).

Reports for 1963 and 1964 record more students than could be accommodated in the Hostel and, in 1965, that there were so many people working at Knossos that some had to be put up (by previous agreement with the Archaeological Service) in the Villa Ariadne. In Athens, accommodation problems were eased by a modest southward extension of the Hostel, built in 1967–8, for which again the architect was Vasiliades.

Peter Megaw (with Electra Megaw), Director 1962–68

Work in the field was extended in both space and time. In Cyrenaica, after a chance find of archaic Greek pottery at Tocra in 1963, the Libyan Department of Antiquities invited the School to join in excavating the site. For two seasons John Boardman and John Hayes, with other BSA students, carried on the work, which was published in two *Supplementary Volumes*. In Cyprus, the School assisted its Director to resume his excavation of the castle at Saranda Colonnes (Paphos), which he had begun before his appointment to Athens. In the North, excavation of the very early Neolithic site of Nea Nikomedeia, in 1963, was followed, after survey work by Eric Higgs, by that of the first Palaeolithic site found in Greece at Asprokhaliko/Kastritsa, in collaboration with Sotirios Dakaris of the Greek Archaeological Service, in 1966 and 1967. Another early dig at Saliagos off Paros, by John Evans and Colin Renfrew (1964–5), documented the neolithic of the Cyclades for the first time. In 1963 on Kythera, George Huxley, Nicolas Coldstream and their team brought to light the first Early Minoan site outside Crete itself; an excavation which was completed in 1965. Popham and Sackett, having finished their limited explorations at Palaikastro, began work in 1964 at the Late Bronze Age and Dark Age site of Lefkandi in Euboea, which was to continue to be of major importance for twenty years — or more. Its selection was a by-product of the Euboea Survey, begun in 1964 and published in *BSA* 61 (1966), one of the first area surveys to be the product of several scholars. Three seasons (1963–5) of cleaning at Perachora prepared the ground for the investigation of those parts of the site not studied by Payne or included in *Perachora* I and II. Lord William Taylour continued to dig at Mycenae, in the Citadel House, and at Ayios Stephanos, alternating excavation with study sessions.

At Knossos, where Hood continued to work on the Palace Plan and up-dating the Survey, as well as his own finds, the Stratigraphical Museum, completed in 1964, was fitted with shelving by the Greek Archaeological Service; Mervyn Popham, Assistant Director since 1963, undertook the transfer and arrangement of its contents with the help of other British scholars. Its formal opening by Dr. Joan Evans, on 2 February 1966, is described below, as are the excavations. The continuing process of survey in the rest of Crete (Hood, Warren, Cadogan and others) produced a new site for excavation in the south of the island, the Early Minoan settlement of Phournou Korifi near Myrtos. This was cleared by Peter Warren in three campaigns between 1967 and 1959, and published with admirable promptitude. The excavation of its neighbour, Myrtos Pyrgos, by Gerald Cadogan belongs to the next decade.

Students of the School were also involved in the rescue excavations in Elis in areas due to be flooded by the Peneios barrage.

The removal of the Greek Antiquities Service from the Ministry of Education to the Cabinet Office, in 1960, was followed by rapid expansion and not infrequent re-organisation. One result was the closer relationship between the Director and senior students of the School and the growing staff of Greek archaeologists in the Service. But such benefits were to be marred by staff changes for political reasons,

Peter Fraser,
Director 1968–71

which were made wholesale after the Colonels seized power in April 1967. Following the crowded years just recorded, the unsettled conditions under the new regime were reflected by a slight recession in student numbers. By 1970 this prompted serious debate as to the best means to increase interest in the School, whether by broadening the fields of study or by extending its hospitality to foreign students who had no national institution of their own in Athens. The School's title now reverts to 'The British School at Athens' — without 'of Archaeology' which had been introduced in 1935–6 — and its value to other aspects of Classical studies was to be emphasized, partly as the result of the all-round improvement in its library. The devaluation of sterling in November 1967, though alleviated by a supplementary Academy grant, was not conducive to an increase in student numbers, and at the same time new regulations of the Colonels' government began a spiral of increasing expenses in all aspects of life in Greece. Peter Megaw retired from the directorship in 1968, so it was on the shoulders of his successor, Peter Fraser, that the brunt of those difficulties fell. A larger intake of students from the Commonwealth now begins to be noticeable, and the Annual Report for 1971–2 goes out of its way to comment on the remarkable range and variety of topics studied in that session.

The excavation programme suffered no diminution. Work continued on a large scale at Knossos (notably of the Unexplored Mansion) and at Lefkandi; the astonishing House of Idols rewarded Taylour's work at Mycenae. In 1968–70, in Eastern Macedonia the School was part-sponsor, with the University of California at Los Angeles, of work at the very early site of Photolivos, with Colin Renfrew as co-director. In the same year it shared in the survey and part excavation of an under-water site, this time with the Cambridge Underwater Team, at Pavlopetri, in the Elafonisos channel (Laconia). In 1970 began the excavation at Myrtos Pyrgos which was to continue for five years. In Macedonia, the Neolithic and Bronze Age site at Servia, dug in part by Heurtley in 1930, and now threatened by the projected Haliakmon barrage, was the scene of rescue operations, conducted jointly by Aikaterina Romiopoulou and Cressida Ridley, which lasted some years.

The School's premises at Knossos were enlarged by the addition to the Stratigraphical Museum of workrooms, largely financed by a bequest from Piet de Jong (who had died in 1967), and named after him; a cottage was built for the caretaker and the old workroom was transformed into sleeping accommodation. All this was achieved by 1970.

In the autumn of 1971 Peter Fraser returned to Oxford, having personally supervised the improvements to the library which he had formulated in 1967. The compilation of the Union Catalogue of Periodicals, drawn up in collaboration with the Directors of the other foreign Schools and Institutes in Athens, was completed under his eye. His successor in Athens was Hector Catling who, having done a good deal of work with the Oxford Laboratory on the application of scientific techniques to archaeology, early began to urge the establishment of a research unit at the School in Athens. This desirable scheme was for a considerable time held up by the problem of finance; the British Academy was sympathetic, but could not provide the costs of the necessarily expensive equipment and its installation, though it guaranteed to meet the running expenses. In 1973, however, Marc Fitch added to his benefactions by giving £10,000 for the project, which, with contributions from Oxford and other sources, enabled the official opening on 2nd April 1974 of the Marc and Ismene Fitch Laboratory. The first Fellow, Richard Jones, took up his post, after training in Oxford, in May of the same year. In anticipation, it may be added here that a further gift in 1977 of £1,500 from the same source extended the laboratory's facilities, and by 1984 its enlarged staff included two petrologists.

Another new development in Athens was a summer course for undergraduates on the archaeology and topography of Ancient Greece. The initiative came from the Assistant Director, Robin Barber, who organised and led the first course in 1973. Though the political upheavals consequent upon the overthrow of the Colonels' regime in the following summer caused its cancellation for that year, it was resumed in 1975 and has been held successfully — at times in duplicate — every subsequent summer. A course for Classics teachers, organised jointly with the Department of Education and Science, was held at the School in April 1979, and repeated biennially thereafter.

Hector Catling,
Director since 1971

Both old and new sites were the scene of excavations. In 1974 Ken Wardle began work, which was to continue for another nine years, on the tumulus at Assiros Toumba, north of Salonica, primarily to study the Late Bronze Age and Early Iron Age strata. The Director led a return to an old site, the Spartan Menelaion, briefly explored by Dawkins in 1909. Here, in several campaigns, important large Mycenaean buildings, both early and late, were uncovered on the heights behind the shrine, and considerable remains of the LH IIIC period, hitherto unrepresented, except in tombs, in Laconia. New data were collected about the shrine itself, and its dedication to Menelaos and Helen was confirmed by the discovery of inscribed bronzes, themselves of intrinsic artistic merit. Colin Renfrew led a return to one of the School's first sites, Phylakopi in Melos; specific areas explored were that of the Mycenaean Megaron and beside the fortifications on the southeast, where an important late Mycenaean shrine was discovered. At the same time an investigation of obsidian sources and a detailed field survey of the island was conducted by Malcolm Wagstaff, John Cherry and a team mainly from Southampton University; their results are published in *Melos, an Island Polity* (1982).

Emergency excavations in the Knossos area continued almost annually, as new construction in the neighbouring villages and the steady advance southwards of

Heraklion and buildings for the University of Crete brought to light antiquities of every period from Minoan to Roman, and — at the site of the Medical Faculty — early Christian. The post of Knossos Fellow — later Curator — held first by Roger Howell in 1977, then by Jill Carington Smith and after 1980, as Curator, by Sandy MacGillivray proved anything but a sinecure!

Though full excavation in Attica is not allowed to foreign schools, permits were given — as they had been earlier for work on the Dema House (1958–60, Jones, Sackett and Graham) and the country house at Vari (1966, the same team) — for an extensive programme of cleaning in the ore washeries at Agrileza, near the silver mines of Lavrion, directed by Ellis Jones; these occupied several seasons.

Team surveys of a very detailed kind came very much to the fore in these years, and are still continuing at the time of writing. The first of these, except for Melos, was begun by John Bintliff in Boeotia in 1977; it was enlarged to 30 members the following year and renamed the Cambridge-Bradford Survey, under the direction of Anthony Snodgrass. It did not operate in 1983 but resumed in 1984, when 45 pre-modern sites were identified. A field-walking survey of Megalopolis was conducted between 1981 and 1983 by Swansea University College of the University of Wales and the University of Sheffield. An unusual collaborative effort between the School, the Kavalla Ephoreia and the Greek Institute of Oceanographic and Fisheries Research, was a survey of the delta of the River Strymon in 1983. Also in 1983, and arising out of the excavations at the Menelaion, an Anglo-Dutch team, directed by Hector Catling and led by Joost Crouwel and William Cavanagh, began the intensive survey of the area of north-eastern Laconia east of the Eurotas. In 1984 Liverpool University conducted a survey in the Methana peninsula which revealed 33 new sites.

Even before the enlargment of the School's field of operations by the activities of the Fitch Laboratory, the numbers of students had begun to rise again, and the range of their studies to broaden. The session 1974–5 recorded twice as many full students as in the previous year (126 against 62), and in the next both Hostel and Taverna were full in and out of session. By 1980 the Annual Report writes of 'an intractable accommodation problem', with 20 students simultaneously in residence (full students even in the Annexe) in Athens. Artists, *rarae aves* in earlier years, were now found at the School, and an anthropological or sociological tinge appeared more often among the topics of research. Changes in the domestic life of the hostel belong to a later chapter, but the retirement of Jane Rabnett in 1975 must find its place here; some part of the general appreciation of her 25 years devoted service as School secretary in Athens was shown by the conferment on her of the M.B.E.

The quality of life was diminished not only by the smog itself which, by the end of the 70s was a serious affliction to all Athenians, but by new tall extensions built in 1980 to the Marasleion School on the west and to the already lofty Evangelismos Hospital to the south, which created a 'pool' of smog in the School temenos, and by 1982 was seriously affecting the health of some residents. The earthquake of

February 1981, however, left the School substantially unscathed.

Revived and very important excavations at Lefkandi, now conducted jointly with the Greek Archaeological Service by Sackett and Popham, followed the accidental discovery, in 1980, of a Dark Age Heroon of unprecedented wealth and scale. Warren's excavations at Knossos to the north of the Stratigraphical Museum complex, intended to clear the area for a possible extension, proved of such interest that the area was left open, while the question of an extension elsewhere was left pending. In Epirus, the excavation of a late Palaeolithic cave-shelter at Klithi was begun in 1983 and continued the following year.

An Athenian oasis; the School (centre foreground) dwarfed by the Evangelismos hospital, 1962

One hundred years ago the British School in Athens had an ample but uncultivated site, a single building, a director, and two students. Its endowment was small, its support from the British Government nil. But the faith and vision of all those involved in its foundation have found justification at every stage of those hundred years in the achievements of its members and their extended influence, through their dispersion to the museums, universities and schools of many countries, and in the enlargement and perpetuation of Greek studies. Today the School's property is one of the lungs of Athens, its buildings officially preserved as part of the city's heritage. Its place in the learned world, in Athens and elsewhere, is honoured and secure. It is supported by the British Government on a scale undreamed of by its founders; a symbol of this support was the award, in 1980, of the O.B.E. to its Director, Hector Catling, accompanied by that of the B.E.M. to its technician, Petros Petrakis.

Chapter II

The School in London

(A) MANAGEMENT

The work for which the School was founded is mainly carried on in Greece, but its ultimate directing force is the Managing Committee in London. The Committee elects its officers, approves its activities, is responsible for securing adequate financing for the running of the School, and allots its resources. In theory it is responsible to the subscribers who elect, at their Annual Meeting, a proportion of its members and, when vacancies occur, the three Trustees in whom the School's property is vested. In theory, because in fact no occasion is recorded upon which the Annual Meeting did other than approve the nominations submitted to it, or receive without comment the Annual Reports and Accounts set before it.

The first two Chairmen of the Committee, G. A. Macmillan and Professor J. L. Myres, were in office for long periods, Macmillan (after being first Hon. Treasurer, then Hon. Secretary) from 1903 to 1933, Myres from 1933 to 1947. Each saw the School through the difficulties of a world war, each exercised somewhat autocratically the powers of direction and decision which his dedication to, and vast experience of, the School's interests gave him. On his retirement for health reasons Sir John Myres became the School's first and only President; the title of Vice-President continues, illogically, to be given *honoris causa* to benefactors, including successive British Ambassadors to Greece. With the growth of the School the responsibilities of the Chairman have become steadily more arduous and time-consuming. Since 1968, therefore, Chairmen have been elected for a period of not more than four years.

Universities and colleges, the Hellenic Society, the Royal Institute of British Architects are typical of the subscribing bodies entitled to a representative on the Managing Committee, while the British Academy is always represented. Since 1971 there have been two members elected by students of not more than five years standing. The Treasurer is an essential and very active member of the Committee, as is the co-editor (with the Director) of the Annual. Naturally enough a high proportion of members are (and always have been) academics, many of them old students of the School. Elected members retire in rotation, without instant re-election, appointed members often serve for long periods; their cumulative value to the School has been very great and much appreciated.

53

The School has indeed been fortunate in its Treasurers. Walter Leaf, banker and Homeric scholar, held the post until he became a Trustee in 1903; his personal generosity continued until his death. Vincent Yorke, an old student, managed the School's finances for fifty difficult years, twice (at least) tiding it over near-bankruptcy by interest-free loans. H. E. Kneen and Michael Baird were notable for their forceful presentation to the British Academy of the School's case — not always fully admitted — for increased support. In somewhat easier times Owen Meyer, Stacy Waddy and Clifford Stevens have handled greatly increased and more complex business with great efficiency and devotion. Special sub-committees on finance, publications and excavations and so on have proved necessary to cope with the volume of School business; immediately after the war a small Executive committee, recommended by the retiring Director Gerard Young, sat for a few years, but its functions were soon reabsorbed by the full committee.

For many years the School shared its secretary with the Hellenic Society, for a time with the British School at Rome as well, since one day a week was enough to deal with the business of each. Most of the secretaries after Macmillan were old students; William Loring, 1897 to 1903 (with some years out during war service in South Africa); John Baker-Penoyre, who devoted all his time to the three societies, and was the first salaried secretary, from 1903 until 1920, except for a few years of leave or illness during which Amy Hutton took over his work. Next Maurice Thompson (a change from Prehistoric Thessaly), and after 1927 W. R. Lefanu, whose reminiscences of his contemporaneous work for the Hellenic Society have added to this historian's pleasure. Office equipment was clearly minimal, and the Minute books were handwritten until July 1966; the historian's gratitude for the legibility, often elegance, of the hand-writing of successive secretaries may be imagined! For three years (1934–7), R. D. Barnett combined the secretaryship with his work in the British Museum. He was succeeded by Edith Clay who worked on a part-time more or less voluntary basis until 1946, after which she became, in 1948, the first full-time secretary. In her twenty-five years service she became an indispensable source of information for Committee, Directors and students alike. Joan Thornton her successor, who had worked with her for two years, showed in her own ten years service a knowledge of people and school affairs almost as encyclopaedic; Shelagh Meade was for a short time secretary in London and then moved to Athens; Sally Bicknell, appointed in 1975, retired after five years to get married. The present secretary, Elizabeth Waywell, is the first old student to work in the London office since Barnett.

In the beginning, the School's affairs were run from premises, shared with the Hellenic Society, at the Royal Asiatic Society's headquarters in Albemarle Street. With the Hellenic Society, the School moved in 1925 to Bloomsbury Square, and then to 50 Bedford Square, and finally in 1958, under the auspices of the University of London, to that concentrated powerhouse of classical and archaeological studies, 31–34 Gordon Square.

Before the revolution in communications brought by the international telephone and frequent and easy air mail and travel, London and Athens were kept in touch only by rather slow and often unreliable letter post. Once a year or so the Director returned to England; more rarely, the Chairman or secretary would visit the School in Athens. There was scope for misunderstandings, especially as the tight Committee control over expenditure, enforced by the School's slender financial resources, left successive directors with little latitude to make even quite small alterations to matters in their charge. With the advent of easy air travel the School's officials are much more frequently in personal contact and critical matters can be dealt with instantly by telephone; moreover the institution of Visiting Fellow has been especially beneficial in this context, since the Fellow has three months to see the School in action and is thus eminently suited to interpret between Athens and London should the need arise.

The subscribers, many of whom nowadays also visit the School, meet the Committee and each other at the Annual Meeting, held since 1960 at the Royal Geographical Society, previously in the Academy Rooms in Burlington Gardens and earlier still in the Society of Antiquaries, when they hear a lecture on current excavations or other aspects of the School's work. Other lectures are held from time to time at Gordon Square. The Jubilee of 1936 was celebrated with an exhibition in November at Burlington House; this was also shown at the Universities of Edinburgh and Manchester. The centenary is being celebrated on an even more extensive scale.

(B) FINANCE

When the establishment of a British School of Archaeology at Athens was first mooted it was made quite clear by the government of the day that no public money could be expected. After the meeting at St. James's Palace in 1883, when the scheme became definite, an appeal was launched for support, directed at Universities, schools and interested individuals; the Appeal Committee, of which G. A. Macmillan was treasurer, estimated the amount required as an endowment of £20,000, to give an annual income of at least £800; the Director's salary was to be not less than £500, and the first building was expected to cost some £3,000. By June 1885 £4,000 had been raised, and building begun on the site provided by the Greek Government. Among the large subscriptions were those of the Hellenic Society and Oxford University.

The lack of adequate capital was severely felt throughout the first eight or nine years; by 1890 even payment of the Director's salary was in doubt, and Ernest Gardner was only able to carry on thanks to subventions from his College (Gonville and Caius). In 1895 a fresh appeal was made to the Treasury, supported by a long list of signatures of representatives of the British Museum, the Royal Academy, the National Gallery, the Royal Society, the Royal Institute of British Architects, the

Society of Antiquaries, the Society of Dilettanti, the Hellenic Society, and all leading Universities and public schools. This time the Treasury responded with an annual grant of £500 for the next five years. A second meeting called by the Prince of Wales at St. James's Palace in July of the same year, 'with the object of improving the School's financial position', resulted in donations of £1,460 and £375 in new subscriptions, including one from the University of Cambridge. By this 'second founding' both the building of the Hostel and the production of the *Annual* were made possible.

The Government grant was renewed, at the School's request, each quinquennium, but not without enquiry into the amount raised by subscriptions. It is with rather wry amusement that a student of political *mores* reads Mr. Asquith's words from the Chair at the Annual Meeting of 1900: 'It is not a splendid sum for the richest country in the world to contribute in support of the efforts of British scholarship to hold its own in a field in which other and poorer countries have for long put us to shame, both in the scale of their operations and by the munificence of their expenditure. But I imagine that the choice lay not between £500 a year and a larger or more adequate figure, but between £500 a year and nothing at all', and then remembers that Mr. Asquith's own government, a few years later, took no steps to improve this provision! This had risen to £917 by 1905, but never topped the £1,000 mark until 1937/8. By this time and from these resources there were two buildings to maintain (the building of the Hostel having been largely financed by another appeal), a growing library to keep up and extend, School studentships (two originally, later one) to fund, and an Assistant Director's salary to be paid; the Treasury grant was adhibited to the Director's salary. Architects too were needed for excavation work; several of these also worked for Evans at Knossos. There was also the publication of the *Annual*, which was already in deficit by its third issue. Not surprisingly, excavations were largely financed by special funds and subscriptions. In 1899 the Cretan Exploration Fund was set up, under the joint administration of Evans and the School Director (Hogarth); a certain amount of this naturally went to support Evans' work at Knossos, but it was also used to finance the School digs at Praisos and Palaikastro. A special appeal was issued for Sparta, which proved an expensive site but was well subscribed. In 1907 the Byzantine Research and Publications fund was established, in association with the School.

Except for the *Annual*, expenditure in London was minimal. The Secretaryship was shared with the Hellenic Society, and was even so on a part-time basis. Treasurers, first Walter Leaf, then Vincent Yorke, acted in an honorary capacity, the editors of the *Annual* received honoraria only. Small sums were paid to the Royal Asiatic Society for the use of its premises in Albemarle Street, and later, after the joint moves to Bloomsbury Square and then to 50 Bedford Square, to the Hellenic Society for office space and clerical assistance.

Annual Reports and Accounts show by what narrow margins each School session ended in credit or deficit. Even small-scale expenditure, on the garden or servants' wages, had to be controlled by the Committee, since even small extravagances could put out this delicate balance. Adjustments to Hostel charges for rent or food had also to be approved in London. In spite of this stringent housekeeping the School and all its activities grew and prospered until the 1914–18 war. During these years, though money was saved on the studentship, in abeyance throughout, subscriptions inevitably fell off, to as low as £600 in 1919. For a time even the continuance of the Government's £500 was in doubt; in 1917 responsibility for its payment was temporarily assumed by the Foreign Office, in recognition of the Director's services to the Legation and the use made of the Hostel to accommodate officers and persons in Government service. It reverted to the Treasury in 1921, but a request to double it was refused. Grounds and building, like servants' wages and all essential services, became increasingly costly to maintain; the *Annual* became thinner and covered more than one session.

In 1916 a piece of land on the opposite side of Odos Spevsippou, the property of Mone Petraki, was put up for sale. It was clearly desirable for the British and American Schools to acquire this if possible, but it was initially sold at auction at a price beyond their means. In 1918, however, it was expropriated by the Greek Government, who also paid three-eighths of the cost, in favour of the two Schools, who were thus able to afford to buy it. By the terms of the expropriation not more than one house was to be put up by each School, and the land built over was not to exceed one-third of the total area; the rest was to be partly afforested, partly turned into a garden; no resale was to be permitted without the permission of the Ministry of Religion, and the Monastery's water-supply was to be safeguarded. After the war a wall was erected by each School round its plot, but the British School was in no position to do more to make use of it. In 1926 the 'Splendid Gift' of the Gennadion Library was completed at the east end of the (larger) American share. Schemes were mooted to build a Hostel for women students, British as well as American, first by Miss Virginia Gildersleeve, Dean of Barnard College (New York), for the International Federation of University Women, and later by the Women's Hostel Committee of the American School. Participation in these schemes was rejected by the Committee; British women students had in any case been admitted as residents in the Hostel since 1920. But it was clear that the School was not going to be in a position to make use of its new possession; after negotiation the plot was sold in 1926 to the Chairman and Director of the American School — who had altered it plans to cater for accommodation for both sexes — and Loring Hall became the School's new and handsome neighbour.

The Annual Report for 1921/2 notes a marked increase in the number of foreign students admitted, remarking wryly that 'it is a matter for regret that a corresponding increase in the support given to the School at home cannot be recorded'. In fact, in an expensive post-war world it was back to less than its pre-war financial resources. One new large subscriber appeared the next year when the Commissioners for the 1851 Exhibition (always strong supporters of the School at Rome) began to give £200 annually. In 1924 the Treasurer 'drew the attention of the (Annual) Meeting to the serious financial position of the School. The necessary and long over-due repairs to the Director's house (the roof had been damaged in a fire) would make serious inroads upon the small capital the School possessed, and unless further subscriptions could be obtained the activities of the School in future would have to be curtailed'. In July 1925 Mr. Yorke offered to lend £300 to the School to tide it over a particularly bad patch; the salaries of Director and Assistant Director were due, and the School had no balance at the bank. The Secretary (Maurice Thompson) who had recently been in Athens, told the Committee 'the School appeared to be most efficient. What had struck him most was the extent of the School's activities and the most inadequate financial support. . . by the colleges of Oxford and Cambridge'. Of those activities the Mycenae and Sparta digs were financed by the usual appeals and private generosity. Heurtley's excavations in Macedonia drew on a Macedonia Exploration Fund. (An appeal for such a fund was issued in 1912. In 1919 a letter from the British Association for the Advancement of Science appointed a committee including Wace, as Director of the School, to promote the excavation of early sites in Macedonia. There seems to be no record of how much money it had.) In 1929, they were supported by the British Academy.

The great acquisition of this period, Evans' gift of Knossos, was intended by him to be self-financing, with an endowment of £3,606, rents from the estate supporting its upkeep and with a large proportion of the Curator's salary guaranteed by himself. When the Taverna fell into disrepair he had it rebuilt at his own expense. In the event, in spite of constant trouble over estate tenants (with which the Committee in London was not really well-equipped, by distance if nothing else, to deal), the degree to which Knossos became a serious drain on the School's finances did not become apparent until well after the war.

Subscriptions were raised in 1929, and in 1930 the Committee once again approached the Treasury, asking for a modest increase in the annual grant to £750; this was refused, but the Treasury undertook to renew the £500 indefinitely, without review or reapplication. An appeal to the Pilgim Trust was also unsuccessful. It is not surprising that in the following year the Committee decided it could no longer afford to have an Assistant Director; Heurtley left to work in Palestine, and part of his duties devolved upon a Senior Student. The post was restored in 1935. The Perachora excavations were insulated from these financial straits by a large anonymous donation.

The 1936 Jubilee Appeal brought satisfactory responses both from the Treasury, who at last raised the annual grant to £1,000, and from the public, in the form of new subscriptions, life compositions, and nearly £1,200 in donations. On this firmer basis, and the Director's generosity, the Payne library was added, both buildings were modernised, the garden beautified. A further bonus was the stabilisation of the drachma/pound exchange rate, which lasted from 1936 to the German occupation. The wild fluctuations of the previous twelve years had added considerably to the problems of running the School, and caused hardship to the students. There were to be parallel problems during the post-war decades.

For several years after the School resumed its work in 1946 its funds were drawn through the Embassy, an arrangement which at first disguised, then aggravated, its financial problems. In spite of larger Treasury grants, £2,000 in 1946, £4,000 in 1948, by January 1949 £4,000 was owed to the Embassy against a bank balance of £2,000. By the following year the Foreign Office was asking for repayment of £6,600; £2,740 worth of investments were realised and the Treasurer loaned £5,000, once again saving the School from bankruptcy.

It was in these grave circumstances that the British Academy became the channel through which all British Schools and Institutes abroad (not including those of the British Council) were to be funded. (A similar role was played vis-à-vis scientific learned societies by the Royal Society.) Estimates were to be submitted to, and allocations made through, the Secretary of the Academy, then Sir Mortimer Wheeler; the estimates were to be triennial, the allocations annual. The system was adopted in 1950/51, and is firmly established. One of its first effects was the relinquishment of Knossos, which had become a financial millstone — in 1949/50 its net cost to School funds was £1,749.

The academy 'umbrella', with its system of comparability between archaeological institutions was, after 1964, to become one of very great benefit to all concerned. It implied general acceptance of standards for salaries which, tied to British university scales, would increase without having to be fought for, of grants for excavation and research made as a matter of principle. In the early years, however, things did not always go smoothly; the School's estimates were challenged, some of its applications refused, and it was not absolved from the need to make special efforts, outside the system, to raise money for capital expenditure, such as the 1959 Library extension. Financing the Hostel, especially when inflation in Greece and in Britain were out of balance, had a central intractable problem; if rents and food costs in Greece were high, students could not afford to stay for a full session; if the Hostel had too few residents its losses in British terms became unacceptable. For some years a policy was adopted of filling the Hostel and Annexe to capacity, during the tourist season, with casual students and visitors for the sake of the rents — a policy partly self-defeating because of staff problems and increased wear and tear.

The grants rose annually throughout the 1950s, but could not keep pace with requirements. Writing in 1959, the Treasurer pointed out that 'the School buildings are old and do not approach modern standards in such matters as heating and sanitation', adding that no major renewals and replacements had been made in the Hostel since 1947. (A special grant of £1,000 for replacing the library roof had been made in 1933. The Upper House servants still had a *pieds-de-géant* lavatory (in good working order) in the late 1950s!).

In 1961 necessary capital repairs, and an accumulating adverse balance as grants fell short of requirements, made it necessary to sell £5,000 worth of securities; on paper the School was insolvent. One Visiting Fellow (Robert

Hopper) commented on the Government's 'obligation to enable the School to hold its own and perform its functions in a proper manner. . . the shame lies not in accepting government help but in allowing the poverty-stricken state of the School to continue without energetic protest. I may add that foreign friends, even Greeks, commented on this to me'. An encouraging feature of these years was the number of Universities and other institutions which greatly increased their subscriptions, in some cases well over the level necessary to secure representation on the Committee. (for example, the Royal Commission for the Exhibition of 1851, whose annual grant had doubled by 1975). Against this, individual subscribers became less numerous as the heavy cost of producing the *Annual* came to be reflected in increased rates of subscription.

At the 1964 meeting between the Academy and representatives of British Schools and Institutes abroad not only were generous basic principles for their support agreed, but formal recognition was given to the disparity between the resources available to them and those of equivalent foreign institutions, a disparity long ago commented on by Sir Richard Jebb. The German Institute in Athens, for example, which had no expenses in Germany since these were covered by the parent Institute, had some £37,000 a year, including £8,000 for excavation; the BSA figure for 1964/5 was £15,000. The easier situation after this meeting was upset by the British devaluation of 1967 — partly compensated by an increase in grant — and new Greek legislation which was estimated to add some £1,000 a year to the Athens wages bill. At the next meeting, with the Academy in 1969, extra provision was agreed to include some £3,000 for 'surveys and research', £1,000 for buying books, and help with publishing *BSA*. Support for the series of Supplementary Volumes, begun in 1966, was already agreed.

Thereafter a steady rise in grant is recorded in Annual Reports. In 1974 the Academy agreed to meet the running costs of the new Fitch Laboratory, in 1979/80 to give £10,000 towards supplementary publications. In recent years substantial additional grants have been made for specified purposes. World-wide inflation, the oil crisis, steep wage increases resulting from Greek legislation and unstable exchange rates continue to combine to cause anxiety to the School's Treasurer; finance for excavations and their publication is still sought from outside bodies; but the fundamental needs of the School are now met by a scale of Government financing which enable it to function with dignity and on a scale undreamed of in its early years. *Pourvu que ça dure!*

It would be churlish not to acknowledge, with warm gratitude, the many benefactions made to the School, in addition to the steady and faithful support of the subscribers which has been its life-blood. Many of the major items find their mention in the various sections of this history — the gifts of Knossos, of the Finlay library, of the Fitch Laboratory, of the Stratigraphical Museum, of the Macmillan Studentship and large subventions to the library. Others, like the very large sum lately given by Cosmo Rodewald, have not yet found a distinctive use. What cannot be expressed, but will never be forgotten, is the multitude of ways in which the School's friends, students and others, have, with often repeated gifts, aided its work, promoted its publication, embellished its premises or contributed in timely fashion to the comfort of its members.

(C) PUBLICATIONS

In view of its close association with the Society for Hellenic Studies it was natural for the School, in its early years, to look upon the Society's *Journal* as the natural place to publish its work. Early excavations were reported in it; those at Megalopolis and Phylakopi were published as *JHS* Supplementary Volumes. To this day *Archaeological Reports* are produced under the aegis of both bodies. After the 'second founding' of 1895, however, it was decided that the School should — like similar bodies — produce its own *Annual*, partly in order to make a better return to subscribers, who had thitherto received only Annual Reports. The *Annual* was first envisaged as as a rather light-weight periodical, to contain short articles and progress reports, while more solid matter was still destined for the *JHS*. A large part in converting the *Annual* into the main School organ was played by the publication in it, from 1900 to 1906, of Evans' annual reports of the excavations at Knossos. Material so novel and so important needed to be balanced by equally weighty matter; more especially, as the School was excavating mainly in Crete at the time, the value of having all Minoan material together was evident. Archaeological studies, even on Bronze Age topics (which might then have been deemed non-Hellenic!), continued to appear from time to time in *JHS* — 'Minyan Ware', for instance as late as 1915 — but it became School policy that work done under its aegis should if possible appear first in the *Annual*.

As a good 'house journal' the *BSA* used to include Annual reports and Accounts, as well as the proceedings of the Annual Meeting, and a cumulative list of students arranged by year of first entry. Since 1935 the separate publication of the Annual Report has left more room for purely archaeological matter, and provided a measure of economy, since the Report requires no illustrations; it also makes possible two tariffs for subscribers, for those who do or do not receive *BSA*. There is cause for regret that the long roll-call of students appears no more, but the annual intake is now so numerous as to preclude its inclusion. Shorn of these ephemera the Annual has emerged as one of the most austerely professional of archaeological journals; even book reviews find no place in it. Mention should perhaps be made here of its value in obtaining, by regular exchange, other periodicals for the library.

The School Director is ex officio one of the editors of *BSA*; the other, based in Britain, is naturally responsible for the practical side of publication. This heavy responsibility, its scope seldom appreciated by contributors, has been carried for a surprisingly long time by each editor in turn. From the beginning, editors and Committee have been dogged by financial worries; as early as *BSA* 3 (1897), Cecil Smith lent the School £50 to tide publication over a sticky patch. By 1908 the

Annual's gross cost had risen, over six years, from one-seventh to one-fifth of the total income of the School, and a limit of 400 pages for any one issue was proposed. During the 1914–15 war there was little material to be published and joint numbers were issued; but *BSA* 23 (1919), containing preponderantly work done in Macedonia by old students in the Salonica Force, was so expensive that the next was held over for a session as an economy measure. The financial aspects of the heavy Mycenae number, *BSA* 25 (1923), seem to be unrecorded. From this time, issue of the *Annual* slipped gradually into arrear; remedies were discussed in 1935, but hardly had time to take effect (and were delayed by the Myres *Festschrift*, *BSA* 37 (1940)) before the outbreak of war. Post-war Annuals have appeared yearly with remarkable regularity and with very high standards of presentation, in spite of steeply rising costs. Complete *Festschrift* volumes are no longer published — the last, for Wace on completing 50 years work in archaeology, was *BSA* 46 (1951) — but a regular number may be dedicated to a distinguished scholar, as was *BSA* 60 (1965) to Ashmole, or be prefaced by an Address, usually in Greek, often in verse, in honour of some sister institution for centenary or other celebrations.

Since 1966, the publication of lengthy excavation reports and extended special studies in the form of Supplementary Volumes (assisted often by special grants from university or other sources) has speeded up the appearance of new work in the Annual. From the same year dates the reproduction of older volumes by the Kraus Reprint Company.

Before this, very large-scale excavations were published in different formats. As late as 1929, *Artemis Orthia* (Dawkins, et al.) which had been delayed by the war, was published by the Hellenic Society. *Perachora*, left inchoate by Payne's sudden death, appeared in two large volumes — heavyweights indeed, described by one reviewer as 'the last of the battleships' — the first edited by Dunbabin from Payne's MS, in 1940, the second, largely also produced by him with the collaboration of many School students, but finally brought to publication, after his death, by Martin Robertson, in 1962. The cost of these was defrayed by an anonymous donor (who had already contributed generously to the excavations) by whose wish they appeared as a separate publication. *Unpublished objects from Palaikastro*, in *BSA* format, had appeared as Supplementary Paper No. 1 as early as 1923. *Fortetsa* (the Cretan tombs from Proto-geometric to Orientalising dug by Payne and Blakeway in 1933–4), was brought out as No. 2 in 1954 by James Brock, who had also taken part in the excavation. The series of post-war campaigns at Mycenae, by Wace and others, published in articles in succeeding Annuals, has now been consolidated into a single Supplementary Volume (No. 12; partly financed by a timely legacy from Gisela Richter). It was at one time hoped that this could be done for the Ithaca excavations of the 1930s also, but means were not forthcoming. A list of Supplementary Volumes to date is given in Appendix VII.

'Archaeological Reports' were in the early years a regular feature of *JHS*, under the title 'Archaeology in Greece'. The first, a short appendix written by Penrose, appeared in *JHS* 8 (1887), the second, a fuller account by Jane Harrison, in *JHS* 9

(1888) . Thereafter they were contributed by School Directors, for whom their compilation has remained an important, time-consuming (and often burdensome) part of their work. From the first *Annual* to the 35th, the Reports were included in them; from 1935 to 1954–5 they reverted to *JHS* (coupled with the Annual Report). After 1955, rechristened *Archaeological Reports*, redesigned and enlarged, they became a joint publication of the School and the Society, and later acquired their own editor. More up to date, though less full, than the *Chronika* of the *Archaiologikon Deltion*, easier to use than the *BCH* 'Chronique des Fouilles' or the *AJA* 'Newsletter from Greece', they keep their readers abreast of archaeological developments in Greece and regularly include valuable summaries of progress in kindred areas.

The *Annual Report* to subscribers appears in time to be available at the February Annual Meeting in London; usually it includes the Treasurer's accounts, though in some years these were printed separately. Besides the summary of the session's main events in Athens, in the field and in the library, the Report gives a list of the year's full students and their work in hand, and obituaries of old students; these, like the records — never again we hope — of the war service of old students, formerly appeared in the *Annual*.

Though not strictly a School publication, the 1906 *Catalogue of the Sparta Museum* (Tod and Wace) originated with Bosanquet. Its success prompted an invitation from the Greek Archaeological Service to the School to catalogue the Athens Acropolis Museum. The Catalogue of the Sculptures duly appeared, with School backing: Vol. I (Guy Dickins) in 1912, Vol. II (Stanley Casson) in 1920. Since then museum catalogues have naturally been in Greek hands. At Knossos, however, before the hand-over, John Pendlebury produced both the *Guide to the Stratigraphic Collection* (1932), which was also issued as a pamphlet, and the *Guide to the Palace of Minos* (1933); this was later republished in Greek in *Kretika Chronika* (1950) and also in a new English edition (1954, reprinted again in 1969).

Chapter III

The School in Greece

(A) ATHENS: THE BUILDINGS

If the School's head is in London, its body, and above all its heart, is in Athens. It is amusing to recall that, at an early period in its history, it was seriously suggested by a well-wisher that, in place of a central establishment at Athens, it would be better if the funds could be devoted to providing a peripatetic yacht for its accommodation. The site originally assigned by the Greek Government was on so generous a scale that it has easily accommodated the expanding buildings of one hundred years and still has enough garden space to provide an oasis in the crowded Athens of today. Its boundary with the American School of Classical Studies on the east is hardly marked by physical barriers, and the tennis court (made in 1906 on American initiative) is shared between them. On the west, a strip, at one time designed as a section of Aristodemos Street but early rendered useless by being blocked, at the lower end, by the Evangelismos Hospital, was walled off (in 1892–3) at either end by the School to prevent its use as a refuse pit — or worse — and formally joined to the School property by Royal Decree in 1907 (beyond, Spevisippou/Souedias Street a small chasm used to proceed uphill under the name of Aristodemos Street; in the thirties it had a convenient kapheneion where trictrac could be played on summer evenings, but it now climbs tidily for several blocks until it meets the pine-woods of Lycabettus).

The Upper House has changed little in appearance since 1886 except in the domestic out-buildings to its north. Within, successive Directors have adapted its accommodation to their own needs, since the creation of the Hostel made the housing of students exceptional — as in 1946/7 — and the Library emptied the large *saloni* of books, and left it free for formal entertaining.

In the Hostel, accommodation for full-time students is much the same as, though infinitely more comfortable than, when it was first built in 1897, with little cast iron grates for coal fires (still used in the 1930s for special reasons or persons), long since replaced by oil-fired central heating; with the two rooms added at the north end during the erection of the Penrose Library, it provided room for 12 students on one floor, a common room (the Finlay Library), dining-room and Library at ground level, and domestic offices in the semi-basement. Two small rooms on either side of the entrance hall have had a variety of uses; the Jebb Room, which housed the

*The Upper House
from the south, 1983*

eponymous collection of photographs, became the School Office, the Ladies' Room
— in any case rendered obsolete when women were admitted to residence —
became the Library Office. The balcony outside the Finlay Library, a great
amenity at all seasons, was added in 1905 at the expense of Cecil Harcourt Smith; it
was designed, like the Library, by Heaton Comyn.

When the numbers of shorter-stay students seemed set to grow, in the 1950s,
more accommodation was provided outside the Hostel proper, to the north. Here
in 1942 the Swiss Red Cross had erected one-storey 'sheds' against the terrace wall
of the Upper House to house their relief stores. Their removal was at one time
mooted, but instead they were re-roofed in tile and made usable, first as a studio for
the artist Antony Baynes, then, in 1950/1, entirely re-conditioned plumbed and
furnished to make three dormitories (since converted to single rooms). In 1956 a
flat for the Assistant Director was constructed on top of them, thus releasing a room
in the Hostel and giving the Assistant Director more scope for family life and for
entertainment.

It is not surprising that, with the very large numbers of students annually
admitted in recent years, accommodation has often been 'an intractable problem'.
But students travel, come and go at different times, and nowadays have no
difficulty in finding accommodation elsewhere. Books on the other hand, once
admitted, remain, and *their* accommodation has made necessary very nearly all the

The Annexe with Assistant
Director's flat above, 1983

major enlargements of the Hostel to date, and seems likely to go on doing so. The L-shaped Penrose Library was added at the north end in 1904, to enable the existing books to be moved from the Director's house and to provide more space. In 1937 the large Payne Room was added to the west of the Penrose Library; 30 feet north-south, 22 feet east-west, it gave more room not only for books but for readers. At the same time, an annexe up a short flight of stairs from the main library, to the north, provided a new room for maps, photographs (including Payne's own collection) and the School's small collection of antiquities; beneath it an *apotheke* (storeroom) was constructed to house excavation gear and students' effects; this had been noted as a *desideratum* since at least 1920.

By 1950 the books were pushing again, but the addition of 200 feet of 'attic' shelving in both parts of the Library gave a respite. Since the library roof had to be reconstructed in the next year, as a matter of urgency, it would have been difficult to find funds to build. In 1959 the *apotheke* was converted into a Periodicals Room; new constructions against the western *temenos* wall provided replacement storage as well as a workshop for the vase-mender. The growth of the Library was hastened, after 1960, by large-scale acquisitions made to fill the *lacunae* noted by Peter Fraser, and by an ever-expanding intake of periodicals. The sherd collection was moved to the western annexes in 1961/2 to make more room for the growing collection of maps in the 'Museum'. In 1964, under the architectural eye of Peter Megaw, plans were drawn up for a much larger addition to the library, which was to provide not only more book space and another reading-room, but a new museum and photo-archive room, and a much needed dark-room. The lower level, reserved for future extension of the periodical stack rooms, was left open temporarily as a carport. Thanks to a noble gift of £5,000 from I. D. Margary, and generous response elsewhere, the addition was put in hand in the summer of 1965 and completed within the year. This does not end the story of the Library's expansion, for 1973 saw the expected extension of the periodicals stack. Now the books are looking upward for more space, and some of them will celebrate the School's centenary in a new home built over the one-storey section of the Penrose Library and the Payne Room.

With the mid-sixties press of students, the old dining-room was often uncomfortably crowded. It was also clearly desirable that Visiting Fellows should have their own quarters, private but not separated from the life of the Hostel. The all-round growth of administration, too, made imperative more office space, particularly for the Director, whose existing office was in the Upper House, for the Assistant Director, who had none, and for the School Secretary. These requirements, already envisaged in 1937 by Gerard Mackworth Young, were comprehensively met by an extension at the southern end of the Hostel, containing one office and a dining-room at ground level, with a three-roomed flat above, reached from the main staircase but slightly below the bedroom floor level; the old dining-room provided the other offices, and laundry and boiler rooms were added

The Hostel with extension at the south, 1983

at the bottom level. The old secretary's office was converted into a visitors' sittingroom.

Both north and south entrances were modified in 1969 to admit cars. The last major changes were due to the Fitch Laboratory which was installed in 1974 in the former store-room adjacent to the mender's workshop against the western wall. It consisted initially of instrument room and dark room, but soon began the inevitable process of expansion, and in four years took over the workroom for petrological studies. The vase-mender and the larger pieces of sculpture were found a new home under the Finlay balcony.

This is not the place to go in any detail into the external embellishments or internal improvements in the School buildings. Considering the modest cost and the speed of their construction, both buildings have stood up well to the passage of time. Twice the Upper House roof needed extensive repairs, in 1900 when Penrose had to supply a new design and specifications because his original plan had not been properly executed, and in 1924 when a chimney fire was narrowly prevented from spreading. After the re-plumbing, partial central-heating and general embellishment of both houses and the garden, undertaken in 1937 by Young largely at his own expense, it was said with truth that 'the utility, condition, and appearance of the School buildings and premises are already much improved, and need not fear comparison, when the work is complete, with any other foreign school in Athens'. But after the war much was to do again; decorations grow dingy, heating systems wear out; standards change and, as one Visiting Fellow remarked, 'there is no virtue in discomfort'. New Government regulations concerning domestic hours and wages made the installation of labour-saving devices, set on foot by the enlightened forethought of Mervyn Popham when Assistant Director, as much a matter of good house-keeping in Athens as in England.

The garden was first laid out 'at private cost' — a phrase which may conceal the identity of Bosanquet, whose life-long interest in the School garden is commemorated by the grey marble *exedra*, designed by H. M. Fletcher, erected from his bequest 'to provide something of lasting beauty and dignity in the garden'. Heaton Comyn's plans for the Penrose Library included a suggested layout for the western part of the *temenos* which however seems not to have been adopted, since this area has long been occupied by the Aleppo pines which give shade to the Hostel and are of considerable age — they were certainly mature by 1980. At all periods directors, students, and latterly their wives, have planted and cared for the garden. Winifred Lamb wrote: 'Wild Flowers, both rare and common, had been planted and flourished in every conceivable corner, anemones, crocuses, periwinkles, tulips. All the proper garden flowers were there too, and the violets beyond the Finlay balcony were almost as large as pansies. Students added small collections of their own, which often occasioned disputes over territory; had Henrietta planted her *Crocus Thomasianus* on the top of Henry's rarer *Tulipa Hageri*? Enthusiasm was undoubtedly stimulated by the admission of a botanical student, Miss Lindsell, in 1928 and the following year.

'During part of Payne's Directorate, work in the Hostel garden was more or less handed over to the Hostel inmates, at their request, with excellent results. One of their number was entrusted with a sum of money, collected by subscription, for the acquisition of extra plants, which were bought either at the Botanic Gardens or in the Sunday flower market outside Ayia Eirene.'

Young was responsible for the flagged path, flanked with oleanders, from the Upper to the Lower House; nowadays the oleanders have given place to acanthus. In wars or their aftermath vegetables were grown in the flower beds, and chickens were kept to help with the food supply (one cock was sacrificed in response to student complaints in 1947, another caused strong protests from American students in the early 1950s). In 1951 the garden received a legacy of £500 from William Miller (his dog's grave is near the western wall). Much replanting, notably of flowering trees, was undertaken by John Cook after the second war; he also introduced as gardener George Kyriazopoulos, who has now completed nearly 40 years' service in this capacity.

In recent years the garden has been transformed by the discovery of a tough grass which, with only a modest amount of irrigation, remains green all the year round. Especial grace is thereby added to the beautiful pistachio and orange trees of the Upper House terrace. Although a not inconsiderable area is now inevitably required for car-parking, and in spite of the extra buildings, the garden, one of the very few of its size in Athens, continues to provide scope for large scale entertainment, either for conferences, such as the International Conference of South-East European Studies in 1970, or, in combination with the American School garden, the 1982 International Classical Conference, or for celebrations like the Jubilee party in 1936. It was regularly the scene of the Director's annual garden-party, formerly reported in the social columns of the Greek press. Its preservation, with that of the buildings, is now the concern, as part of the heritage of Athens, of both the Greek Department of the Environment and the *Ephoreia Neoteron Mnemeion.*

(B) ATHENS: THE LIBRARY AND COLLECTIONS

For the first eighteen years or so the library was contained in the large north room of the Upper House. The first large increase in its holdings came in 1890, with the gift of £400 from the Newton Memorial Fund. By 1897 there were enough books for a printed catalogue to be prepared, and for the Director (Cecil Smith) to be in consultation with the heads of the French School and the German Institute over common library policy. By 1901 space was running short, and Smith, now returned to the British Museum, gave a sum of money towards building a library in the Hostel. After Penrose died in February 1903, it was felt that his services to archaeology might fittingly be commemorated by the erection of a library at the

School, and the funds raised were devoted to this end. Plans were prepared by Heaton Comyn the School architect, and completed, under his supervision, in time for the formal opening of the building by Crown Prince Constantine during the 1905 Archaeological Congress; a memorial tablet to Penrose was placed over the fireplace, and his bust, executed by an Athenian artist, was presented by the Greek Archaeological Society. The University Presses of Oxford and Cambridge responded to requests to mark the occasion with gifts of books. By 1907 the rearrangement of the books (earlier begun by Marcus Tod, the first librarian) was substantially complete. It follows its own system, as is proper for a specialist library, which is not the least of its assets for those using it. The Topographical Index, begun under Harcourt Smith, has also been of great value to generations of scholars.

The annexe built at the same time as the Payne Room provided space for maps, for the sherds and other antiquities previously housed in a small room off the entrance hall, and for the photographic collection. This, first mentioned in the records in 1908, had two large accessions in 1937 in Dilys Powell's gift of Payne's photographs and papers and in the 150 given in his uncle's name by Sir Richard Jebb's nephew, and then totalled 3,438 catalogued items. Another large accession was a collection of air photographs presented in 1949 by the British School at Rome; its arrangement and cataloguing, a considerable undertaking, was the work of John Boardman. Over the years the collection has been steadily enlarged by excavation archives, including negatives, and the legacies of scholars like Winifred Lamb and Vincent Desborough.

The collection of maps, which includes valuable early maps like those of the *Expédition Scientifique de la Morée* and the nineteenth-century Austrian General Staff series, acquired the War Office General Staff Geographical Section sheets after the war, and is constantly being brought up to date.

The sherd collection was begun by Gardner in 1891, shortly after Petrie's visit to Athens. After his excavation at Amarna, Petrie gave 42 sherds to the collection, and also his notebook of water-colour drawings of pottery (the basis for the illustrations in *Tell el Amarna*) which is preserved in the School library. In 1937 the sherds were catalogued and rearranged before moving into their new quarters; much enlarged, the collection was reorganised and moved to the western *apotheke* in 1962, only to be transferred to the new museum in 1966. As a study collection and record of surface exploration it is of unique value. Some antiquities were included with the gift of the Finlay Library. Others were acquired thanks to a legacy from Ernest Gardner, who died in 1939. Doreen Dunbabin gave to the School a number of vases and terracottas her husband had collected. The largest single acquisition was made in 1956 when 80 vases and terracottas from the Empedokles Collection were chosen for the School by the Archaeological Council. All these collections have benefited from the devoted work, in mounting, cataloguing etc., of many hands, notably those of the wives of Assistant Directors, Visiting Fellows and students.

The library suffered no damage during the war. Its use as Press Office until April 1941, while not preventing archaeological study, helped to keep the books dry and in good order, and under the occupation first the Americans and then the Swiss kept the books safe under lock and key. In 1946 came the 800 or so books selected by Dunbabin from the library of Sir Arthur Evans, some of which were passed on to Knossos, where the library at the Villa had been seriously depleted by the Germans. The backlog of books and periodicals, held up by the war, began to flow in, and new periodicals, exchanges with the *Annual*, started to multiply.

The acquisition of the books necessary to fill the gaps noted by Peter Fraser took time and search, this to a large extent carried out by himself. His recommendations also concerned purchasing policy, and the general running of the library. The primary responsibility for acquiring books still lay with the Assistant Director, who however had many other duties, which increased with student numbers and Greek legislation, as well as his own work.

By this time (1960/1) the yearly intake of periodicals had risen to 250, and the library was described as 'in the heavyweight class'. More help was clearly needed, but at first it could only be provided on an *ad hoc* basis. Philip Sherrard spent a year as Librarian after ceasing to be Assistant Director, wives of students were occasionally employed in the library; Mercy Seiradakis (Money-Coutts), now resident in Athens, gave three days a week for the next eight years. In the session 1966/7 Peter Fraser updated his review, which made it clear that more staff was essential. The first full-time Library Assistant was appointed in 1970; this was Babette Young, who was promoted to Deputy Librarian in 1977, and retired in 1981, to be succeeded by Penny Wilson. In 1979 the British Academy made a special grant of £10,000 for the Library, and by 1981 its holdings had doubled, to over 50,000 volumes, within twenty years.

One source of accessions has always been the members of the School, who regularly give copies of their books and articles on publication; theses may also be lodged there. The private libraries of old students are often given or bequeathed, in whole or in part; Bernard Ashmole has given two sets of books, including a notable collection of Loeb texts. Some of Pendlebury's books and papers have passed to Knossos; some of Winifred Lamb's books and papers and all Desborough's books, papers and offprints have gone to the School. Excavation notebooks and records, as well as the photographs already mentioned, form a valuable and increasing part of the School archives.

The Finlay Library is among the School's most treasured possessions. It was presented to the School in 1899 by George Finlay's nephew, G. H. Cooke, together with its shelves, and installed in the Common Room to which it gave its name. In accepting this generous gift (which also included some antiquities) the Committee offered 'to keep the books as a separate collection with an inscription (on the chimney-breast) recording the circumstances under which they were acquired'.

During 1915 and 1916 Wace and Hasluck made use of such spare time as their official duties allowed to reorganise the library and more fully catalogue the books

(Wace) and papers (Hasluck). The Finlay books were not accessible to Hostel residents during that war. The cataloguing of the Finlay papers was continued and completed from 1920–1922 by F. W. Welch, an old student, then in service as Vice-Consul. From 1939 to 1941 hostel residents had access to the books, but these were then removed to the main library for the duration of the war (for Robin Burn's graphic account of their discovery there see above, Chapter I). Their commercial value had by this time greatly increased, and after a serious case of theft some of the more valuable volumes were removed to the safety of the office; they had been rearranged and recatalogued in 1951 to 1953. Later, some of the more valuable items were placed in locked shelving. Over a period of years the books and bindings were treated, conservation measures were applied to the papers (by Veronica Babington Smith, coming from the library of the Victoria and Albert Museum), and a full catalogue was produced by Professor Joan Hussey and published as *Supplementary Volume* no.9. The newspapers from the Finlay collection were lodged in the Gennadion Library.

(C) THE MARC AND ISMENE FITCH LABORATORY

Developments in archaeological science — Archaeometry — were quick to be reflected in the School's work, so that no excavation undertaken by the School since the second world war failed to include some specialised study of material undertaken by archaeological scientists. Students and members of the School were also prominent in promoting the application of laboratory techniques to specific archaeological problems, not least R. M. Cook, in collaboration with J. Belshé (archaeomagnetism); C. Renfrew with J. Dixon and J. R. Cann (obsidian characterisation); H. W. Catling with the Oxford University Research Laboratory for Archaeology and the History of Art (RLAHA) (composition and provenance of Late Bronze Age pottery in the East Mediterranean).

When Catling became Director in 1971, he explored the possibility of establishing a small research laboratory in the School which could exploit to the full the advantages to Archaeometry of working in Greece side by side with interested archaeologists and in immediate reach of the material under study. Preliminary advice was given by the Director and Deputy Director of RLAHA, Dr (now Professor) E. T. Hall and Dr (also now Professor) M. J. Aitken on the necessary resources of space, personnel and equipment. The scheme was explained to Dr Sp. Marinatos, Inspector-General of the Archaeological Service; the Ministry of Culture's blessing was received not long afterwards, and the Managing Committee agreed to try to realise the scheme.

From the first, the School enjoyed the incalculable benefit of RLAHA support and advice, which included gifts of expensive equipment and expertise in recruiting staff. Gifts were made by the Worshipful Company of Goldsmiths, Arthur Guinness Son and Co. Ltd. and by the Oxford Craven Committee, but the minimum capital necessary to convert an existing building in Athens and acquire major items of equipment still seemed remote. Then, in mid-1973, suddenly and characteristically, all difficulties evaporated when Dr and Mrs Marc Fitch, already substantial benefactors of the School, offered £10,000 for the establishment of the Research Laboratory on condition that the recurrent running expenses could be guaranteed in some other fashion. The British Academy, which had shown much interest in the scheme from its inception, undertook to meet these, and the way was clear. Dr and Mrs Fitch were asked, and agreed, to allow the Laboratory to bear their name.

The rest of 1973 and part of 1974 passed in appointing a Research Officer to run the Laboratory, in converting and furnishing the former western *apotheke*, and in obtaining major items of equipment and arranging their transport to Athens. Before the end of 1973 Dr. Richard E. Jones had accepted appointment as Research Officer,and had been temporarily attached to the RLAHA for training in the special techniques that he was to use when established in Athens. By May 1974 he had moved to Athens and the equipment had arrived safely at the School and awaited installation and preliminary testing. Finally, at a brief ceremony on 29 November 1974, the British Ambassador in Athens, Mr (now Sir) Brooks Richards formally opened the Laboratory.

The Laboratory's original complement of equipment consisted of an optical emission spectrograph, an X-ray fluorescent spectrometer ('Isoprobe') and a proton magnetometer, each instrument selected for its particular suitability to the objectives of the Laboratory — the emission spectrograph for chemical analysis of pottery, the 'Isoprobe' (which could be used either in the Laboratory or conveyed by car for use in Museums anywhere in Greece) for the non-destructive analysis of artefacts, especially of metal, the magnetometer for geo-physical prospection in the field. The Laboratory's first few years saw Richard Jones apply all three techniques to problems chiefly generated within the School itself, notably among its current excavations and studies of excavated material. From late in 1974 a laboratory Assistant was employed to deal with the more routine aspects of the work of the Laboratory.

It was understood from the outset that the Laboratory would concentrate on pottery analysis, inheriting in the process the substantial bank of data already built up for the Aegean by the RLAHA and responding to the research interests of members of the School working on problems of origin of Minoan and Mycenaean pottery, as well as certain Dark Age fabrics. The first programmes of analysis were concerned with Mycenaean and contemporary wares from the School's excavations at the Menelaion, Sparta, and with the Minoanizing pottery from the Ayios Stephanos site in South Lakonia. During these first years encouraging results were obtained with the 'Isoprobe'. A wide selection of the Late Minoan bronzes from the School's excavation at the Unexplored Mansion, Knossos (1967–1973) were analysed to study the relationship between type of alloy and object-function. Evidence suggested that the Minoan founders knew their business. A similar study of metal objects from the Lefkandi Dark Age cemeteries was published in M. R. Popham, et al., *Lefkandi* I.

More controversial was the re-opening of the question of origin of the storage stirrup jars inscribed in the Linear B script found by Keramopoullos in Thebes. RLAHA's work in 1964–65, with which Catling had been associated, had suggested an East Cretan origin for many of the jars analysed. This publication had been much criticised for procedural shortcomings: some of these were acknowledged and, in a later paper a West Cretan origin was proposed instead of the original suggestion (*Archaeometry* 9 (1965); 19 (1977)). This was followed by a much larger investigation of incribed stirrup jars from several sites, the results of which appeared in *BSA* 75 (1980), where evidence was published that endorsed the view that many inscribed stirrup jars came from W. Crete, perhaps from Khania. Four authors contributed to the report — a Linear B expert (J. T. Killen), an archaeologist (H. W. Catling), a chemist (R. E. Jones) and an archaeological statistician (J. Cherry). The contribution of the last named in applying sophisticated techniques of data analysis to the results was a most important innovation, and helped to make this paper something of a classic.

From early days the Laboratory has worked in collaboration with Greek scientists. The first venture in association involved analysis, for the Corinth excavations, of Corinthian B transport amphorae by spectrographic analysis; collaboration with Greek scientists was also a feature of a very large project which studied the pigments, plasters and painting technique used in Minoan frescoes. The report was published in *BSA* 72 (1977). Such collaboration has continued on a regular basis with Greek scientists in the Nuclear Research Centre, 'Demokritos', in the Geological Institute and other bodies, and has been an important and welcome consequence of the Laboratory's existence.

Equally gratifying has been the interest aroused among Greek archaeologists and archaeologists in the other Foreign Schools, so that other collaborative projects have also been stimulated in this way. The most far-reaching in its consequences for the Laboratory has been with the American Corinth excavation under its Director Mr C. K. Williams II who became at once collaborator and benefactor, establishing a two year fellowship in petrology and evoking the first substantial expansion of the Laboratory, where, early in 1979, a second room in the block it occupies was converted into a petrological laboratory. Once more Dr Fitch offered help with equipment, giving the polarising microscope used to examine the thin sections prepared from pottery samples. This time the Laboratory was able to pay from its own contingency fund for the conversion and for subsidiary equipment required in petrological analysis. Ian Whitbread (Bristol University) was elected the first Fellow in Petrology, taking up his appointment late in 1979. Throughout the tenure of his Fellowship he worked chiefly on material from the American excavations at Corinth. Mr Williams has continued a generous benefactor, and funded a second two-year Petrology Fellowship for 1984–1986 as well as giving a Hewlett Packard 85 computer for use in the Laboratory.

Inter-School collaboration has been particularly successful in the field of geophysical prospection. The first considerable venture took Richard Jones to Amathus in Cyprus where he made a magnetometer survey for the French School, later to Thasos to help in the search for potters' kilns, a task to which he returned in 1984 with the same French colleagues. On an initiative of the Canadian Institute, the Fitch Laboratory shared with the Canadians in the puchase of a Resistivity Meter and Epson HX–20 computer as a preliminary to a very successful field project at Ancient Stymphalos in 1983 and 1984.

Chemical analysis of pottery by optical emission spectroscopy continued to be the Laboratory's chief activity, so that several, very diverse, projects in addition to those already mentioned were successfully followed through to publication. A pioneering study of Byzantine pottery was initiated by Megaw, published by Jones and Megaw in *BSA* 78 (1983).

In 1979 the Managing Committee acknowledged the contribution of R. E. Jones to the success of the Laboratory by changing his appointment from Research Officer to Director of the Fitch Laboratory. It became apparent that, although optical emission spectoscopy had undoubtedly proved its value, a different technique using more sophisticated equipment could undoubtedly refine and improve results. Once again Dr Marc Fitch was to turn an aspiration into achievement, giving the Laboratory a very large sum with which to buy a Pye-Unicam Atomic Absorption Spectrometer. The British Academy was also very generous, making a substantial grant towards the cost of building a preparation room equipped with a fume cupboard, and providing the emoluments for a Laboratory Fellow (Miss Helen Hatcher, seconded from RLAHA) to assist Dr Jones for a year in establishing the new equipment and bringing it to 'project-pitch'.

At the end of Miss Hatcher's Fellowship the British Academy were unable to fund an immediate successor. After an interval, the Laboratory, again with help from Dr Marc Fitch, produced the emoluments for a second Laboratory Fellow to work on a pottery analysis project stimulated by Professor Nicolas Coldstream's work on the North Cemetery excavation at Knossos of the 1970's.

The second Fellow in Petrology, Peter Day (Southampton University), took up his appointment in February 1984 to make a study of the fabrics of late Minoan pithoi. Ian Whitbread returned to work on his own research concerning transport amphorae of the Archaic and later periods, extending beyond his original area of work at Corinth to all major transport amphora classes in the Aegean.

Throughout these years the Laboratory has taken every opportunity to enlarge its data-bank of clay analyses from the Aegean world, absorbing information from projects undertaken, and reacting promptly to suggestions for the analysis of important representative collections, such as the Archaic pottery from Delos and Rhenia. This, with data already assembled in Oxford, and with the assistance of computer facilities in Oxford and Athens, has taken it some way along the path of creating a 'clay map' of ancient Greece, which has already proved of importance in elucidating problems of provenance in periods from the Prehistoric to the Byzantine. Richard Jones' *Greek and Cypriot Pottery, A Review of Scientific Studies* (1986) surveys the work done in Athens and Oxford, comparing it with that undertaken in other laboratories, and for the first time presents a comprehensive picture of scholarship in this field, where the School can justly claim to have been one of the pioneers.

In January 1981 the Laboratory organised a one day meeting in the School at which Greek and foreign archaeologists and scientists gave papers on a variety of topics connected with Archaeometry in Greece; the papers evoked good discussion and comment, and the event brought together archaeologists and scientists who normally have little opportunity for meeting. A second meeting, with an attendance of well over 100, was held two years later; the Laboratory was delighted to welcome Professor E. T Hall from RLAHA who both gave a paper and summed up at the end of the day. The Laboratory looks forward to holding such meetings regularly every two years.

The Laboratory's publication record to date has been creditable; most projects are reported in *BSA*, *Archaeometry*, or *Journal of Field Archaeology*, but not a little important work has been subsumed by excavation reports.

Ten years after the opening of the Fitch Laboratory it can be seen as a successful enterprise that has benefited from wide support and interest, both from the School itself, from its principal benefactors, Dr and Mrs Marc Fitch, and, more recently, Mr C. K. Williams, from the British Academy and, very particularly, from the Oxford RLAHA. It takes some pride in its unique position, and believes it has successfully demonstrated the importance to Archaeometry of the closest possible collaboration between archaeologists and scientists. It is also proud of its record as a focus of collaboration between Greek, British and foreign archaeologists and scientists and of having played a not insignificant role in the evolution of Archaeometry in Greece.

(D) RELATIONSHIPS

The School's buildings and major assets have now been described, the names of some who have lived and worked in it have flitted across its annals, and its achievements are to be sketched, at least, in subsequent chapters. To define its character, however, is not an easy exercise, but must be undertaken before its relationships in Greece can be considered. Not easy, because from its inception, within the framework of its Regulations, the School has been self-creating — a similar phenomenon at the American School of Classical Studies is described by Louis E. Lord in his *History of the American School of Classical Studies, 1882–1942* (1947). After Penrose, the average period in office of each director was six years, often less; the majority were comparatively young men, most of whom had gained their experience and expertise as students in the School. Each of course had a special interest in some aspect of archaeology, but all had to be equipped with the wider knowledge which would enable them to advise their diverse students and to meet the challenge of excavation. The students, admitted for their promise over a very wide field, came mostly fresh from university, in the early years mainly from Oxford and Cambridge, and were admitted on recommendation. Only the School Student(s) of each year, and later the Macmillan Student, were appointed by the School, and the former were selected by the Vice-Chancellors of their universities. From their interactions, especially during the winter months in Athens, the School acquired its *ethos*. In this, financial stringency played an important part; a frugal independence has always been a notable feature of that *ethos*. The lack (previous to the acquisition of Knossos) of a permanent excavation site meant that a larger proportion of British students in Athens than of other nationalities was at liberty to pursue their own individual studies except when a large-scale excavation, such as Sparta, involved them in a communal project. Yet this independence has not separated the Directors from their students, nor prevented the creation of a corporate entity which, however much it may vary in emphasis from period to period, is recognisable and familiar across the generations. Much of this, in a naturally unhierarchical society, has been due to the qualities of the successive Assistant Directors (listed in Appendix V), whose influence, based on daily shared living, was not less for being seldom expressed. This comes out particularly clearly in the reminiscences of people who were at the School during Heurtley's long tenure of the post.

Except at the official level it is hard to express the relationships of a body so diverse in age and background, in subject of study and attainment. Accordingly its relationships on this level will take pride of place.

Very little material survives from which to form any impression of the School's external relationships in Athens in its early years. It is safe to assume that Greek archaeologists and the other foreign Schools were welcoming and helpful, and that the Legation did much to promote the well-being and influence of this other British lien with the life of Greece. In existing records there is, surprisingly, no mention of the installation, in 1887, of the American School of Classical Studies on its present site, though the existence of such a neighbour must have been as welcome then as it has been since. The heads of the foreign schools were in frequent contact, and as early as 1896 they agreed upon unity of action in regard to library purchases and catalogues. Mutual access to each other's libraries (and to the outstanding photographic archive of the German Institute) was normal and easy, as was attendance at each other's courses of lectures. At one point British students were invited to go on the organised American 'School trips' which took place early in each session, and American students were put up in the Hostel during repairs to their own School in the first war.

Congratulatory addresses, usually in Greek, often in verse, were addressed to other Schools, at Jubilee or centenary, as well as to appropriate Greek authorities on numerous occasions. On the occasion of the Athens Archaeological Congress in

1905, for example, 'a Joint Address from the Hellenic Society and the BSA, drawn up by Sir Richard Jebb' was presented to King George of the Hellenes; other addresses greeted the 75th Anniversary of Athens University in 1912 (presented by Hasluck, Assistant Director, composed by Marcus Tod and illuminated on vellum by Walter George), at its centenary (attended by the Chairman and addressed by the Director, who received a Greek decoration), and at the Byron centenary celebrations in Athens and Missolonghi, when the Hon. Treasurer, the Director and Assistant Director were all honoured. An Athens University celebration in 1909 of the birth of Gladstone — his bust stands outside it — was the occasion of unofficial congratulations by four School students (Wace, Ormerod, Thompson and Zimmern) who arrived in a taxi with wreath and poem in eight lines of elegiacs, and were later felicitated on their initiative by the Committee.

The Annual Report for 1905/6 records 'this session has witnessed a further development in social intercourse between the Archaeological Schools. Receptions were given during the winter at each School in turn, and students had opportunities of meeting one another and making the acquaintance of Greek and foreign residents'. This pleasant practice fell victim to the 1914–18 war, but 'American teas' were a notable feature of winters in the 1930s, and the open house kept in those days at 9 Ploutarchou by the Hills and Blegens fulfilled much the same function on a smaller scale.

The Bosanquets were on close and friendly terms with the Egertons (HM Minister and his wife) and the School was much involved in the public events and functions of 1905 and 1906 — the Archaeological Congress and the Olympic Games, at which Bosanquet (at the request of the Board of Education) was the official UK representative. The School was regularly involved in the British Royal visits of those years — sometimes at very short notice! — and the Director escorted the King to Acropolis and Museums. British athletes were put up in the Hostel and allowed to use its libraries.

During the first war, as during the second, the School became an adjunct of the Legation; its director became a Government servant, the Hostel was mainly occupied by persons on Government business or in the armed forces. But after the first war the tie slackened, and seems almost, during the 1920s, to have been non-existent. Apart from learned persons like William Miller, historian of Mediaeval Greece, who came regularly to use the libraries, the School seems to have had few acquaintances among British residents except the members of the Copais Company, whose hospitality in Boeotia was generous and appreciated. No doubt successive British Ministers kept a benevolent eye on the School through the political upheavals of the times, for in June 1936, during the preliminaries to the founding of the Byron Chair at Athens University, Sir Sidney Waterlow met the representatives of the School and the nascent British Council to discuss how, if at all, the Council could be of assistance to the School. It was natural that the appointment of Gerard Young (and the darkening international situation) should draw the School closer to the Legation; at the same time the daily presence in the

Secretary's office of Ruby Woodley, a resident of long standing, and the move of the Anglo-Hellenic League (and above all its friendly administrator, Mrs. Irene Hadjilazarou) to a nearby site, gave opportunities for contacts with the British colony which, naturally, intensified during 1939–41.

Since 1946 School Directors have been ex officio Honorary Attachés at the Embassy, and successive Ambassadors have become, as Vice-Presidents, members of the Managing Committee — a position which is well merited by the constant interest and assistance extended to the School, though anomalous as there is no President. In the first post-war years the School depended on the Embassy for drawing money and rations, for postal and customs facilities, for practical help and advice of all kinds. In easier times since, Embassy walks and Christmas Day picnics became a feature of student life.

Relationships with the Greek Ministry of Education and the Archaeological Service are of vital importance to the School. They define the conditions in which archaeological work takes place, manage the museums, make rules for the conduct of excavations. From time to time the rules may be changed; the obligation to buy and present to the Greek State the site of a projected excavation is at times more leniently interpreted than at others. A general rule that (except for the Americans in the Agora) foreign Schools may not excavate in Attica was generously 'bent' for Vari and Agrileza. The problems of land valuation are amusingly described by Cecil Smith in *BSA* 3 (1897).

In recent years many excavations have been joint projects — Servia, Lefkandi, Debla — and the Greek authorities have called upon the assistance of the foreign schools for urgent rescue excavation, as the work in Elis preparatory to the Peneios barrage. After the first war, Tsountas generously waived his right to dig at Mycenae in favour of the School; from 1950 Greek and British diggers worked independently at Mycenae, but after Wace's death in 1957 the site reverted to overall Greek responsibility, without however preventing continuing work there by Taylour and others. In general terms, the return made by the foreign schools to Greece is chiefly in the objects from excavations which all go to Greek museums. Support for Greek scholars to visit British Universities and Museums is an ambition which it was hoped the Centenary Appeal might enable the British School to satisfy, and has been realised.

Dilys Powell describes (*The Traveller's Journey is done* p. 90) the enthusiasm with which the Athenian 'monde' greeted Payne's more spectacular discoveries, but the fashionable, even the Anglophile, world impinged little upon the ordinary life of the School. A number of serious readers frequented the Library, and there were friends of long standing like Miss Negroponte, who received the formal thanks of the Committee for her kindness to generations of women students, and Mrs Hadjilazarou. In 1926 the Secretary of the Anglo-Hellenic League urged (in a letter) that students might mingle more in Greek society, and Winifred Lamb, to judge from her letters, in fact did so. R. H. Bulmer, by living outside the School, formed a number of non-archaeological social ties; Gerard Young played a notable part in the musical life of Athens. But work, scant means, and constant travelling made it easier for students to dispense with non-archaeological society. Language was no serious barrier, since learning to speak Greek was for most students one of the first priorities. The exigencies of travel soon added a vocabulary and ease learnt by the Direct Method to the fruits of more formal instruction. In their travels, more than in Athens, students were immersed in the ordinary life of Greece, came to accept its rhythms and taboos and the wonderful hospitality for which no return was expected — or, often, possible — but the satisfaction of the hunger to learn something new. One of the incidental pleasures of excavation lies in the daily casual exchanges of views with the workmen, whose grasp of world political issues would put most northerners to shame.

A special place in the life of the School belongs to the foremen and menders, whose years of practical experience far exceed those of most archaeologists. Several will be mentioned in the next chapter. From 1953 Petros Petrakis served as mender and technician until his retirement in 1985; his importance to the School was recognised in 1980 by the award of the B.E.M. His marriage in 1953 to Eleni Kandaraki, the domestic stay of the Directors' households from 1946, meant that she too remained part of the School's life, especially at Knossos.

At home in the Hostel successive housekeepers and domestic staff have provided not only friendly service, often in excess of the calls of duty, but a care for and real interest in the doings of all the residents which has produced the family atmosphere so generally recalled in reminiscences of all periods.

Earlier in the century the Hellenic Travellers were regularly entertained at the School, as were the cruises organised by Ernest Gardner. In the inter-war period Sir Henry Lunn often asked the School to provide on-site guidance for the Travellers, and Heurtley did in fact on several occasions go down to Mycenae to meet the cruisers coming up from Nauplion. Efforts to persuade Sir Henry to subscribe to the School on a regular basis came to nothing, but on several cruises substantial collections were made on board for School funds. It is to be feared that in the later '30s the more irreverent students would go *incognito* to the Acropolis when the cruise ship was in, rather in the spirit of those going to the zoo. This was perhaps only fair; the 1939 excavators at Mycenae, breakfasting in the Grave circle, were the site's star attraction to all tourists of that summer. A story told by Hogarth records that Arthur Evans was showing one or two friends round the Candia Museum when a party of Travellers entered, and some attached themselves to him. After a few minutes the following conversation was heard: one Traveller to another: 'Come away, dear, this is quite the worst Cook's guide we have come across so far'.

Before the last war unofficial visitors to the School were few; a handful of schoolboys, teachers and undergraduates in the Long Vacation. Many of these now attend the summer courses for students, though some still come independently. Since 1950 the numbers of Temporary and Associate students have grown into a flood, far outnumbering the capacity to accommodate them (a fair proportion of these were in fact admitted to work on specific excavations or surveys, and spent little time in Athens). Official visits are of course made from time to time by the Chairman, Secretary, and other members of the Managing Committee. On two occasions the Secretary of the British Academy has been entertained both by the Director and in the Hostel.

(E) KNOSSOS

The School had no permanent interest in Knossos until 1926. Recent research by Mrs Ann Brown, however, on material kindly made available by Dr Nowell Myres, reveals how nearly it was involved there even before Sir Arthur Evans. In 1893 John Myres, already in close touch with Evans at the Ashmolean Museum (where he was Keeper of Antiquities), went to Crete as Craven Fellow, and, after visiting Knossos, sought the approval and support of the School and the Hellenic Society to undertake excavations there. Ernest Gardner, in Athens, warned him of a possible American involvement in the site — the French School too had expressed an interest — but conditional approval was forthcoming from London. In the event, Myres was invited to dig in Cyprus and abandoned his plans for Knossos, though he never lost interest in the site and visited it again with Evans in 1895 and on many subsequent occasions.

The story of Sir Arthur Evans and Knossos has been told in detail by his half-sister, Dr. Joan Evans (*Time and Chance*, 1942), by Dilys Powell (*The Villa Ariadne*, 1973), by Ann Brown (*Evans and the Palace of Minos*, 1983) and by Sylvia Horwitz (*The Find of a Lifetime*, 1981). The School's historian thus needs, here, only to sketch the events of the years between Evans' first involvement with Crete and 1926 when he transferred to the School's ownership the Palace of Minos, the Villa Ariadne, and the estate, mostly under vines, which was to provide the income for their upkeep.

Evans first visited Knossos in 1894, his wife's death the year before having prevented a planned rendezvous there with Myres. The Kephala site's potential importance had long been recognised; Schliemann for one had hoped to dig there but was initially defeated by the complexities of land-ownership and purchase, and died in 1890 before these could be overcome. In 1878/9 a local antiquarian, with the promising name of Minos Kalokairinos, had dug part of the west wing, bringing to light some of the magazines of giant pithoi and the ante-room of the Throne Room, and had made probes in the area later to be identified with the south front of the Palace. Evans was determined to excavate, and as a first step succeeded in buying one quarter of the land, which would in time be a lever for securing the whole. This was not achieved until in 1899 Crete, liberated from Turkish rule, was constituted by the Powers an autonomous state, with Prince George of Greece as High Commissioner.

With the strong support of the established Cretan archaeologists J. Hazzidakis and St. Xanthoudides, who drew up a 'projet de loi' for Cretan antiquities, Evans was granted an excavation permit for Knossos, while other areas were reserved for the British and other foreign schools. With his own funds, supplemented by the newly formed Cretan Exploration Fund, he began to dig in March 1900. Within a week, the first inscribed tablets were brought to light; within a few more, much of the west wing of the Palace, including the Throne Room.

Over the years that followed, until 1913, with Duncan Mackenzie as his assistant, the Swiss Emil Gilliéron (père) as restorer, a succession of architects, Heaton Comyn, Theodore Fyfe, and Christian Doll, and a large team of increasingly competent workmen, Evans uncovered the successive Minoan palaces, with the houses round them, the Little Palace to the west with most of the 'Royal Road' which led to it, and the large cemeteries of Isopata and Zafer Papoura to the north. In 1906, with a mass of material to be studied, he built the Villa Ariadne — its architect was Christian Doll — on rising ground beyond the Heraklion road, to be the residence and working headquarters for himself and his staff. Though major finds were sent to the Heraklion Museum, much of the sherd material was stored in the Palace itself, in what was to be organised by John Pendlebury as a stratigraphical museum.

Knossos, the Villa Ariadne, 1985

After the interruption of archaeological work by the 1914–18 war, and the publication in 1921 of the first volume of *The Palace of Minos*, Evans returned to excavation at Knossos, but already in 1922 he broached the idea of handing over his stake there to the British School. The Deed of Gift was signed on 11 January 1924 at his house, Youlbury, on Boar's Hill, Oxford, the witnesses being Duncan Mackenzie and J. S. Candy, of Blagrove, who gives a delightful picture of life with Evans at Youlbury in his *A Tapestry of Life* (1984). The Deed refers specifically to all the land, the Palace and other sites 'no part of which has been expropriated by the Greek Government, so that it all remains my personal property'. The transfer was formally recognised by a decree of the Greek Ministry of Ecclesiastical and other Affairs dated 26 January 1924. To this splendid gift he added an endowment of £6,800, and a substantial contribution — after the transfer — towards a salary for a Curator. In 1928 he paid for the conversion of the 'Taverna' — a small house at the road end of the Villa drive — into accommodation for members of the School, and when in 1933 it suffered serious damage he paid to rebuild it. Later it became the Curator's house, and people from the School, and privileged visitors, were put up in the Villa. In memory, the semi-basement bedrooms seem dark and gloomy — no electric light then! — though admirably cool in the heat of summer. Sir Arthur slept there unscathed during the 1926 earthquake, when a heavy marble table is remembered as 'dancing' on the terrace.

Evans by no means abandoned Knossos after the hand-over; his visits were frequent, sometimes alarming. On the last of these, the *Lesche* of Heraklion held a three-day festival in his honour, at which he was crowned with bays, and a bronze portrait bust was erected in the West Court of the Palace. Hutchinson reported to the Committee 'Scenes like those represented on the miniature frescoes were reproduced . . . when the Metropolitan of Candia, the Demarch, the Ephor and other officials of Candia assembled to do him honour. Later a wreath was presented to him by the President of the Scientific Society, and the Ephor, Dr Marinatos, delivered an address on the subject of Sir Arthur's achievements'. His old servants stayed on at the Villa, and Manolaki (Emmanuel Akoumianakis, 'the Old Wolf'), foreman of many years, still presided over Knossian archaeology. 1935 also saw the publication of the last volume, IV, of the *The Palace of Minos*; Volume II had appeared, in two parts, in 1928, Volume III in 1930. This truly monumental work bears on almost every page the unmistakeable imprint of his erudition, insight, and personality.

The first Curator, appointed on 13 March, 1926, was Evans' assistant of many years, Duncan Mackenzie, but within a year Evans and the School had agreed that he was not well suited to the post and, in 1929, arteriosclerosis and other weaknesses caused his retirement, first to a clinic in Athens, and then to the care of his sister in Italy. Recent use of his Knossos notebooks has brought out afresh how great was his contribution to Minoan archaeology. His successor, John Pendlebury, young — he was only 25 — international athlete as well as scholar, brought immense vigour and zest to Knossos. In 1931, with his wife Hilda, he was excavating Middle

Minoan Ia houses under the *Koulouras* (pits) of the West Court, and fighting with Evans over the text of his *Guide to the Palace of Minos*. By 1932 he had completed the guide to the Stratigraphical Collection (*Guide to the Stratigraphical Museum in the Palace at Knossos: dating the pottery in the Stratigraphical Museum* Vol. I, by H. W. and J. D. S. Pendlebury; Vol. II, by E. Eccles, M. Money-Coutts and J. D. S. Pendlebury; Vol. III, *the Plans*, by M. Money-Coutts and J. D. S. Pendlebury).

Whenever possible the Pendleburys were walking Crete from end to end, noting sites and routes and collecting the material which went into the making of his comprehensive book, covering all periods, *The Archaeology of Crete*, published in 1939. At Knossos the Curator had also to oversee the management of the estate; the letting of the vineyards caused ructions almost annually, and it must have been with triumph that in 1934 a profit of £90 was reported. An additional parcel of land, the 'Mathioudakis plot', was acquired in 1933 for archaeological reasons.

Part of the Pendleburys' year was spent in Egypt, where they were engaged in excavations at el Amarna. Partly for this reason, the Committee came to feel, with Evans, that more constant supervision at Knossos would be desirable, and that the Curator should be there, or within easy reach, for at least the eight months of the School session. The *immediate* cause for this was the excavation by local authorities, in Pendlebury's absence, of three Middle Minoan tombs. This also showed it to be desirable that the School's sphere at Knossos should be exactly defined, and this was done in 1934. Pendlebury, unwilling to give up Egypt or his freedom to work in other parts of Crete, accordingly resigned, and Richard Hutchinson took over as Curator in October 1934. His nick-name of 'The Squire', acquired at the Mycenae dig, proved apposite indeed for this gentle and immensely learned man. He was a bachelor, but was accompanied almost everywhere by his mother. Their mutual devotion was at times prejudicial to business in hand, and students were often impatient with her conversation, but no-one could fail to admire her courage in facing crippling arthritis and, in 1941, the dangers of war and invasion. The Pendleburys, freed from responsibility for Knossos, turned to excavations in the Lasithi area.

A winter visitor to the main Minoan sites was still likely to have them to himself, but summer tourists were beginning to be numerous. The Department of Antiquities sought — exceptionally for that time — to impose charges for admission to the Palace, though except for the wages of a Guardian all maintenance costs were borne by the School, which held, understandably, that if fees were to be charged they should be allocated to the upkeep of the site. The *Tourismos* erected a 'rest-house' on School property, and then regularised the situation by an *ex post facto* application which offered a peppercorn rent and stated that it claimed no rights. In 1937 the School gave land for a house for the Guardian and, after preliminary excavation, for a car park, and the King of Greece and General Metaxas were entertained at the Villa by the *Tourismos* — to the disgust of the Venezelist domestic staff!

The excavations of these years, extending into 1940, are dealt with below. After the outbreak of war, the Curator did some teaching for the British Council. He was joined in 1940 by John Pendlebury, in name a Vice-Consul, in fact engaged in organising Cretan resistance to the almost inevitable invasion. When it came, in May 1941, both he and Manolaki were killed by the Germans (Dilys Powell, *The Villa Ariadne*). The Hutchinsons, after briefly entertaining the King of Greece at the Villa, on his flight from Athens, were evacuated to Egypt. The School is indebted to Nikolaos Platon, then Ephor in Heraklion, for saving its property in fair condition and for removing the more valuable part of the Villa library (about one third of the remainder was burnt by the Occupying forces) to the safety of the Heraklion Museum.

The Villa became the Headquarters of the German G. O. C. Crete. It was on his return to it one evening in 1944 that General Kreipe was ambushed and carried off to Cairo by Paddy Leigh-Fermor and Stanley Moss (*Ill-met by Moonlight* by Moss is the primary source for this episode, which also finds its place in Powell's *The Villa Ariadne*). When, a few months later, the Germans began to withdraw, the Villa was almost simultaneously 'liberated' by Tom Dunbabin, descending from the mountains, and Manoli Markoyiannakis, one of the pre-war staff, and the position was regularised and any possible further destruction averted by swift action by Platon. The Villa was subsequently taken over by the Commanding Officer of the British Military Mission, and a detachment of Greek troops was stationed in the Taverna. UNNRA was to be represented, but, with German troops still in Khania, Crete was thought to be unsuitable for women. Thanks to Dunbabin's expertise — tested during the Occupation — in the infiltration of personnel, Mercy Money-Coutts and Edith Eccles were introduced from Cairo, and accepted with good grace. At first they shared the Taverna with the soldiers; later they took possession of all of it and made it sufficiently habitable for the Curator's return. Dunbabin, meanwhile, set on foot the re-equipping of the Villa and the restoration of the estate to cultivation, before transferring to Athens as Officer for Monuments and Fine Arts.

When the School re-started in 1946, the Villa was still occupied by the British Liaison Officer with the Military Mission and his family; the former library was reserved for School visitors. The Curator, with the old Villa servants, returned to the Taverna, and general rehabilitation of the site and land was taken in hand, but the Palace, at least, was beyond the School's resources. Even after Piet de Jong, with his many years' experience of Knossos and Minoan architecture, had succeeded as Curator in 1947, other funding was called for. As Ephor of Antiquities for Crete, Platon involved his Ministry in preservation measures for all the Cretan palaces, and Marshall Aid was in due course allocated for archaeological purposes to the Knossos area.

It was however becoming increasingly clear that for financial reasons the School's position at Knossos would not long be tenable. In 1947 the Managing Committee discussed a proposal to hand over the site and the estate to the Greek Government, but decided that this would be contrary to Evans' Deed of Gift.

Piet de Jong at Knossos
(photo, John Boardman)

Another suggestion, made in 1949 by Arnold Toynbee, was for UNESCO to be invited to take over Knossos and run it as an international centre of Cretan and Aegean studies. In spite of remarkably successful estate management by the de Jongs, Knossos was proving too great a drain on the School's resources. As the Chairman wrote to Mortimer Wheeler, 'it costs £2370 a year to run, gross, and all we have to set against this expenditure is Evans' bequest of £240 p.a. [the original lump sum had been converted into this annual figure] and a varying amount from rent and produce of the land, usually about £300'. As the British Academy was not prepared to help, the Palace, Villa and estate were accordingly offered to the Greek Government, and the transfer was agreed for 1952. Only the use of the Taverna (with occasional accommodation for students in the Villa) and the land round it (defined by a new plan prepared by de Jong) was reserved to the School, together with the right to excavate without compensation within the limits defined in 1934. De Jong remained in residence for some months, but as Architect, no longer Curator. A memorial tablet to Evans, in Greek, was put up in the Villa, and for a short time Platon and his wife stayed there, but were driven away by disturbing noises in the small hours (later School residents had reason to attribute these to rats). Later on, however, the Platons stayed regularly at the Villa before and after their season's work at Zakro. The Villa was much used during Hood's major campaigns between 1957 and 1961, and it was done up by the Greeks for the First Cretological Conference in 1961, a date selected as the 1,000th anniversary of the liberation of Crete from the Arabs.

The change of ownership made little difference to the scale of work at Knossos. Since 1950 Sinclair Hood, then Assistant Director, had been digging tombs in the area, in collaboration with de Jong or with St. Alexiou. As Director, he continued to clear tombs of various periods before he embarked on large-scale work beside the Royal Road. A workroom was added to the Taverna, all its facilities were enlarged and its part in the life of the School became ever more important. The richness of Knossos as an area of work was never more apparent than in 1956 and the succeeding years, when excavations from the Neolithic (John Evans in the Central Court), the Bronze Age (Hood's important stratigraphic investigations by the Royal Road, and the Tombs on Gypsades — not to mention tombs at Sellopoulo cleared by Platon and Huxley), Greek (the shrine on Gypsades), and Roman (Michael Gough's work on the Villa Dionysus) were simultaneously in progress. The first comprehensive survey (Hood and Smollett) was made in these years, and published with the assistance of the Council of Management of the Marc Fitch Fund — the first appearance of this benefactor of the School.

Knossos, the Taverna, 1985

More study and storage space was obviously needed. The proposal for a new Stratigraphical Museum, to which could be transferred the Evans material stored in the Palace, came from Platon. Its construction was largely planned by Hood, and to a large extent made possible by donations from Dr Joan Evans and Marc Fitch. Shelving and boxes were provided by the Archaeological Service, and the transfer and arrangement of the material was the work of Mervyn Popham with assistance from others at the School. The opening ceremony, in February 1966, was attended by a large gathering which included many of Evans' former workmen. After an address by Hood, Dr Evans cut a wreath of flowers across the door and declared the building open. A feast followed, for which champagne and raki were generously provided by Dr Evans and Marc Fitch.

From 1964 Knossos became the School's prime site, occupying a high proportion of its students (and not only on excavation), and at times almost monopolising its energies, as during the six-months race against time, in 1978, to clear the site for the University of Crete Medical Faculty, with bulldozers literally at the diggers' heels. Manoli and Ourania Markoyiannakis for many years looked after the School's property and catered for those who worked at Knossos; for many years too, until his death in 1967, Manoli acted as excavation foreman. Another devoted Knossian was Andonis Zidianakis, who began as barrow-boy for Evans during the excavation of the Temple Tomb in 1931; for many years he too acted as excavation foreman, right through until Warren's dig of 1978–1982. A permanent British administrative presence at the Taverna was however seen to be necessary; the post of Knossos Fellow was created, and held by Roger Howell in 1977 and then by Jill Carington-Smith until 1980. The original job of Curator was revived for Sandy MacGillivray in 1980 and retained for his successor, Alan Peatfield, when he transferred to Athens in 1984 as Assistant Director.

By 1969 enlargement of all facilities at Knossos was urgently necesary. A large workroom wing was built onto the Stratigraphical Museum; though planned for Knossos alone, it came to be used by all British diggers in Crete. It was named after Piet de Jong, by whose legacy it was largely funded. The Taverna area was transformed by turning the old work-room into bedrooms, by extra plumbing, by re-housing the library, and the addition of a house for the foreman; the latter now houses the Curator. A further extension to the museum was planned to the west, but Warren's excavations there proved of such interest that it was decided to leave them exposed, and to build, when necessary, on the north.

The museum seems at first sight to contain enough material to provide occupation for generations of archaeologists to come, and closer acquaintance does little to lessen this impression, in spite of the number of people profitably at work in it — nine separate projects in 1984. These have included for much of the year, Petros Petrakis, whose mended pots occupy an impressive amount of shelf space. Labelling and boxing are clear and solid enough to ensure that, for any reasonable amount of time, the material may wait in safety for the students of the future.

Knossos, the Stratigraphical Museum from the Acropolis, 1985

In all this activity the Villa Ariadne now plays little part. It comes to life during Cretological conferences, Platon and other Greek archaeologists sometimes stay there, but at other times it seems to slumber. The trees grow thick and tall about it, and an uncomfortable aura remains from its functions during the Occupation. The teeming tourists who admire the bronze bust of Evans in the Palace of Minos are not encouraged to visit his house across the road. The enchanting dialogues of the octave owls, who used to live in such numbers in its garden, like the competing choirs of nightingales and bull-frogs in the Kairatos valley below, have been — happily not all however — replaced or effaced by amplified music from the discos along the Heraklion road. To this even the Taverna, protected by its trees, bougainvillaea and morning glory from the road, is not completely immune.

Chapter IV

Excavations

Excavation is and has always been the most visible archaeological activity, and the one with the greatest popular appeal. Like medicine, it is both an art and an applied science, including planned campaigns to solve perceived problems or gain new knowledge, and emergency operations to rescue sites in danger of destruction, usually from human action. The School's excavations have ranged in space from Epirus and Macedonia to Naucratis and Tocra (Cyrenaica), from the Ionian Islands to Anatolia (Kusura) and Cyprus, in time from the Palaeolithic, at Klithi and Asprokhaliko, to Mediaeval, at Saranda Kolonnes. Some have been limited campaigns, others were cut short by lack of finance or more complex and varied impediments. Others again, including many for which the School was merely sponsor, continued for years, under successive directors: Rhitsona, near Tanagra, begun by Burrows and continued by the Ures, Ithaca, sponsored by Lord Rennell of Rodd and dug by Heurtley and Sylvia Benton, were of this character; Heurtley's many campaigns in Macedonia, like Winifred Lamb's in the Aegean Islands and Turkey, were not official 'School digs'. Only exceptionally can any site be considered to have been exhaustively cleared, and so the School has often returned, with newer techniques, fresh questions and renewed interests, to old sites, Phylakopi, Palaikastro, Perachora, Sparta and the Menelaion. The Knossos area offered — or demanded — new digging almost annually, a process recently accelerated as Heraklion steadily approached and the sites of new constructions had to be cleared in a hurry.

It would be impossible in a general history of this kind to attempt a full survey of a hundred years of excavations, and both presumptuous and invidious to describe some as more important than others. The few sites here discussed are those at which a major and prolonged effort has been, or is still being, expended, and of these Knossos must be the premier, even though this is to focus too narrowly the School's involvement with Crete and especially Minoan Crete for the whole of this century; Praisos, Lasithi, Palaikastro, Myrtos, Debla can only feature synoptically, on a smaller scale.

As with most aspects of the School's development, finance has been a limiting, often a determining, factor. Appeals, special funds, subventions from bodies like the Society of the Dilettanti, have from the beginning made work possible, and still

Surveying:
Michael Ventris in Chios,
(photo, John Boardman)

do so. A legacy from the American Richard Seager (excavator of Vasiliki, Mochlos and Pseira in eastern Crete), a great friend of Evans and admirer of the School who died in 1924, provided the first excavation fund at the School's sole disposition.

Excavators have always needed to raise funds where they could, by their own efforts. With the more liberal Government financing of recent decades, the School has been able to earmark part of each annual grant for excavation: the Society of Antiquaries of London and Universities have made larger contributions, related in many cases to the involvement of the latter's personnel; thus Birmingham provided money for Tomlinson to dig at Perachora, and Peter Warren by the Royal Road at Knossos.

The site selected, the money found, a permit must be secured. Each foreign school may dig at three sites each year (these include non-School excavations), though extra cleaning permits can exceptionally be granted in addition. Digging may only take place on land owned by the Greek state, so private land must be bought and presented to the State before serious excavation, though trials may be allowed without purchase in the first year, provided that the owner's consent is expressed in a formal legal document. This was not always so; R. P. Austin's dig at Haliartos was on land belonging to the Copais Company, and the Ithaca digs of

1937 and 1938 were on land belonging to Andreas Lekatsas. The Greek authorities may also restrict the areas for which permits can be given; thus, in 1920 foreign schools were asked to confine themselves to sites where they had already worked, and again in 1961 to sites in which they already had an interest. Naturally, certain sites and areas are reserved for Greek excavators; it was by the personal generosity of Christos Tsountas in relinquishing this right for a time that the British were allowed to dig at Mycenae. Except for the American work in the Agora, foreign schools are not usually permitted to excavate in Attica, though even this rule was waived for the small-scale work on the Dema wall and Vari house and the Agrileza ore-washery. Some excavations have been under the joint direction of Greek and British archaeologists — Soterios Dakaris and Higgs at Asprokhaliko and Kastritsa, Aikaterina Romiopoulou with Cressida Ridley at Servia, and the Cemetery excavations at Lefkandi; also Hood with Alexiou, Platon with Huxley, Tsedakis with Warren, all in Crete. Nowadays many Ephors and Epimeletes tend to be closely involved in foreign excavations in their areas. In early days, a small proportion of excavation finds, usually duplicates, might be allotted to foreign museums, but this is no longer the case.

The excavator must now find staff and equipment. Whenever its finances have permitted, the School's staff has included an architect. Some of these, like Christian Doll and Piet de Jong, also worked for Evans at Knossos; de Jong also worked part-time for American excavations. For some years now the School has had an Honorary Surveyor, David Smyth. Often qualified volunteers have come forward to help. Architectural students at other times have made the plans and drawings, and on poorer digs ordinary students learnt to survey and developed skill at drawing. At times various donors have helped the School with surveying instruments. Since its first venture, with the *Sunday Times* expedition, into underwater archaeology, during the Emporio excavations in Chios in 1954, it has also possessed an aqualung, though subsequent underwater exploration has been confined to the northern shores of Crete and Pavlopetri, off SE Laconia. In early years staffing was provided by students; assisting at excavations was, in fact, among the specific duties of the holder of the School Studentship, and the practice is generally continued on 'School' digs. More recently many directors of excavations, especially those concerned with the remoter past, have imported their own teams. However, many students who have spent any length of time at the School have been on at least one dig, and have thus begun to equip themselves to carry out their own excavations later on.

Working on a dig is a taxing operation. Hours are long, intense concentration hour by hour is essential if the essence of the process is not to be lost and mistakes avoided. Of the possible extremes of climatic annoyance, only heavy rain 'stops play'. The Taverna at Knossos is the only permanent dig headquarters; elsewhere accommodation may be either rented or tented. A rented house has the advantage of better shelter, more covered space for workroom and store, lighting and plumbing conveniences of varying modernity and efficiency, and willing hands to

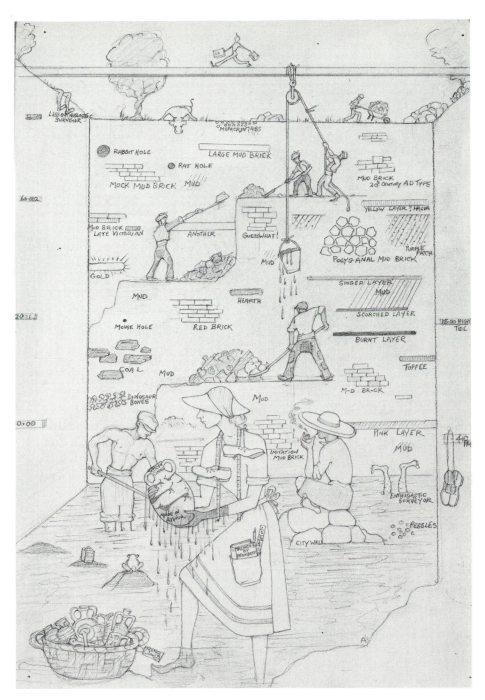

The digger's eye view: Trench B at Old Smyrna, 1949, by Audrey Petty (Corbett);
Ann Jeffery in the foreground.

Manolaki at Knossos
(photo, Vincent Desborough)

perform domestic chores. One drawback may be distance from the site itself; the excavators at Karphi had a long steep climb at the beginning and end of each day, at Myrtos, Phournou Korifi, a 45 minute walk in extreme heat, and even at Mycenae getting about was a perceptible effort in the summer heat. Tents can be pitched conveniently close to the site, and used to make possible a comfortable mid-day siesta. It is wonderful in clement weather to eat and write up the dig-book under the stars, with only the camp cook and *invited* visitors for external company; less satisfactory however when wind sets the canvas flapping and loosens the ropes, or rain puts out the cooking stove. In either set of circumstances, the practical (and psychological) gifts of the directors of expeditions, and particularly their wives, contribute largely to the morale and achievement of all involved, and are long and gratefully remembered. But it must be confessed that few modern excavators and their staffs would tolerate the discomforts cheerfully accepted even 30 years ago.

    Much also is contributed by the dig foremen. Gregorios Antoniou, from Cyprus, worked at most of the School's early sites, and in earlier days also for Evans at Knossos. He is described by Joan Evans (*Time and Chance* p. 340) as 'a superman among foremen, who knew how to keep his men at work and had learned in a *jeunesse orageuse* spent in tomb-robbing in Cyprus how to remove the most 'fragile objects without breaking them'. Peter Megaw visited him in his last years at Larnaca, where he treasured several letters from British excavators of the first generation, in flawless Greek. Of Hogarth (Hogaris to him) he spoke with particular pride, having saved his life, he said, when attacked at Salamis by a two-headed serpent! Manolaki Akoumianakis, his successor at Knossos, is said to have known as much about Minoan archaeology as Evans himself. Still at Knossos, Manoli Markoyannakis, who came from Psychro to work for Evans as postboy, and was afterwards houseboy in the Villa, became foreman after the war. He lacked Manolaki's flair, but was a good organiser, quiet, shrewd, tactful and respected. With his wife Ourania he looked after all who lived at the Taverna until his death in 1967. Antonis Zidianakis, who succeeded him, began as a barrow-boy when Evans and Pendlebury were digging the Temple Tomb. His many years as foreman at Knossos, lasting up to Warren's dig near the Stratigraphical Museum, gave him a surprising knowledge of pottery.

Jannis Katsarakis, who first worked as a mender at Palaikastro with Dawkins (and travelled with him during his war service), was still the School's mender in 1939, having also acted as foreman at Perachora and, in 1937, in Ithaca. His son Stelios followed in his footsteps for a time after the second war. His colleague (and successor) in Ithaca, the red-haired Laetes Moriates, was in complete contrast, though as effective; after a long day (starting at 5.30 am) on the dig, he could be seen setting out for a night's fishing, poised like Poseidon with his trident above the boat's stern light. His Homeric name, characteristic of the island, is the key to the charming story that Sylvia Benton, newly arrived at Stavros, waylaid him with the words 'I wonder if you can help me find your son'.

At Mycenae, the Dases Family provided foremen both in 1939 and after the war. Between whiles they, like Manolaki at Knossos, surveyed their home area with flair and expertise, and passed on their findings to the proper quarters. To students of prehistory their hotel, the 'Fair Helen' at Mycenae, with its collections of books presented by their authors — for they worked also for Swedish excavators in the Argolid — was almost like an offshoot of the School.

(A) KNOSSOS

When Sir Arthur Evans handed over his property at Knossos to the School he had excavated almost the whole of the Palace and its immediate dependencies, some of the houses round it, including the Little Palace and the Royal Villa, and the cemeteries of Zafer Papoura and Isopata, as well as minor antiquities in the area. In later years he also dug the Caravanserai, the House of the High Priest and the Temple Tomb south of the Palace area, and the western approaches to the West Court, besides making many probes to gather fresh data inside the Palace itself.

The School's own involvement with Knossos may be said to date from the setting up in 1899 of the Cretan Excavation Fund, which was to be administered jointly by Evans and the School, represented by Macmillan, Hogarth, and Myres. Thus Hogarth, as Director, was able to dig in 1900 some Minoan houses and a Roman cemetery on Gypsades, and tombs (mainly Geometric) north of the palace; he also did a little excavation — never published — in the southwest corner below the West Court. Thereafter, however, only Evans (with Duncan Mackenzie) dug at Knossos until 1927, when John Forsdyke (later Sir John) excavated a cemetery of Middle and Late Minoan tombs at Mavrospelio on the slope east of the Kairatos, and Humfry Payne, with Alan Blakeway and James Brock, conducted the first of several seasons' work on sub-Minoan and later tombs on the westward slopes of the Acropolis hill in the area of Fortetsa, (these were published in 1957 by Brock as *Supplementary Paper* No. 2). In 1931 the Pendleburys exposed another two *Koulouras* (pits) under the paving of the palace West Court, and the Middle Minoan Houses beneath them. It was at this time too that Pendlebury and his helpers re-organised and catalogued the sherds from Evans' excavations, which were lodged in the west wing near the Throne Room. Sinclair Hood points out that Evans was the pioneer in Greece in keeping a stratigraphic collection of pottery from a major site (as opposed to merely what was acceptable to the local museum), though this is of course now a regular practice.

Before Evans' last visit to Knossos in 1935 steps had been taken to establish the boundaries of the School's excavation area. A fresh survey was made by James Laver, who acted as architect for Pendlebury, and by April 1934 a sub-Committee, consisting of Evans, Myres and Forsdyke, had prepared a report for the Director to put before the Greek authorities. By a Ministerial Note (2958) of 31 August the concession was defined and plans were deposited with the School and the Department. The boundaries were the acropolis ridge to the west, the Ailias hill to the east, the Isopata royal tomb on the north and the Spelia acqueduct on the south.

During Hutchinson's curatorship, work on the Palace was confined to the preservation of the fabric and keeping down the weeds. Elsewhere, Hutchinson made many discoveries, from all periods, including the large Roman Villa Dionysus, later fully excavated by Michael Gough. A survey of Roman remains was made by Raleigh Radford of the School in Rome, but never published. With Tom Dunbabin and a party from the School an 'Archaic' site was explored in 1937 west of the Palace, and a Minoan 'road-junction' on the site of the car-park. In December 1938 the Late Minoan tholos tomb on the Kephala, the first of Mainland type in Crete, was found and, by May 1939, excavated and five tombs of a Proto-geometric cemetery were dug with Dunbabin. In 1940 Hutchinson dug more tombs, a small but rich Late Minoan II Chamber Tomb near the Temple Tomb, and two chamber tombs and a ruined tholos at Khaniale Tekke, which had been re-used in the eighth to sixth centuries; their finds included a house-model and remarkable archaic jewellery.

From 1950 until the present the School's involvement in excavation at Knossos, has been almost uninterrupted, its scale often considerable. Some idea of its growth may be gained by comparing the entries, 169, in the first Knossos Survey, published in 1957, with the 371 of the 1981 up-dating. In the fifties Sinclair Hood was the main excavator, at first in collaboration with de Jong while the latter was still Curator. His work included the digging of Middle and Late Minoan tombs, including the first Middle Minoan tholos of Messara type to be found in the area; years of excavation beside the Royal Road, which confirmed and added to Evans' classification of Minoan chronology, besides the compilation of both the Surveys (the first with David Smollett, the second with David Smyth), and (with William Taylor)of the new detailed plan of the Palace; the tombs were published *pari passu* in the *Annual*, the Surveys and Plan have appeared as Supplementary Volumes. His work on the masons marks from all Knossos excavations is nearing completion.

From 1957 to 1960 John Evans conducted excavations of the Neolithic levels of the Central Court, and in 1969–70 extended these to the West Court also. Investigations on the south side of the Royal Road were carried out from 1971 to 1973 by Peter Warren, who recovered much evidence for Middle Minoan roads and public structures there. From 1978 until 1982 the same scholar dug in the area

Drawing by Piet de Jong
of a vase from a warrior grave
at Knossos

west of the Stratigraphical Museum, to clear the ground for the Museum's possible extension in that direction; in view of the intrinsic interest of his finds, however, it has been decided to leave the area exposed. Apart from the much-discussed evidence of — possibly ritual — cannibalism, the most remarkable remains were three circular built platforms, hitherto unparalleled, which Warren suggests may have been dancing-places.

For several years from 1967, a major effort was devoted to the clearance of the large Minoan building, adjoining the Little Palace, christened by Evans 'the Unexplored Mansion'. The Roman and earlier buildings above it were dug by Hugh Sackett, the Minoan levels by Mervyn Popham. The Minoan Mansion, planned in Late Minoan IA but not occupied until Late Minoan II, devastated by fire at the end of that period and only partially occupied thereafter, was especially notable for the quality of its masonry and the quantities of Late Minoan II pottery. It is now published as *Supplementary Volume* No. 17.

Among Popham's excavations at Knossos between 1967 and 1975, the most productive was that of two rich Late Minoan tombs north of Knossos, at Sellopoulo, where two others, not intact, had been cleared by Platon and George Huxley in 1957. The Stratigraphical Museum and extra work-room space have made it possible for members of the School to tackle important backlogs of publication from pre-war excavations. Gerald Cadogan and David Wilson have been working on Early Minoan, Sandy MacGillivray on Middle Minoan and Popham on Late Minoan II and III pottery, putting knowledge of these periods on a new secure footing.

Knowledge of Greek Knossos was enlarged by the excavation on Gypsades of a sanctuary of Demeter, with many votives of archaic and classical times and a small fifth-century temple (dug by Hood and Nicolas Coldstream, published by the latter as *Supplementary Volume* No. 8 in 1973); and of numerous, mostly Geometric, tombs. These, found and dug at intervals since 1958 — often as rescue operations — have produced some remarkable and unexpected figured pottery. A Hero Shrine, too, whose life extended from the sixth century to the founding of the Roman Colony at Knossos in 67 B.C. should be recorded.

Traces of Roman Knossos, lying nearer the surface, make up a high proportion of the entries in the Knossos Survey, but few have been completely explored. The more notable are studied in Ian Sanders' important book on *Roman Crete* completed before his most untimely death in 1977, but not published until 1982. Besides the Roman buildings over the Unexplored Mansion cleared by Sackett, the only planned dig on any scale was that of the Villa Dionysus; Hutchinson had dug much of this, including the best mosaics, in 1935 (the mosaics suffered severe damage during the war and were repaired in the 1950's by an Italian expert brought in by Platon); the remainder was cleared, in several campaigns between 1957 and 1971, by Michael Gough.

Rescue operations, however, on a very large scale fell to the School, at the request of the Antiquities Service, at the sites of the Venezeleion Hospital and the

Protogeometric vase from Knossos (photo, Nicolas Coldstream)

University of Crete Medical Faculty to the north of Knossos itself. At the first of these sites, an Early Christian Basilica, noted by Hood in 1953, was cleared in several campaigns between 1955 and 1960. It was of aisled type, contained good mosaics, and had been constructed, probably in the sixth century, over probably Christian tombs of which the earliest belonged to the fourth century. West of the Hospital, another Early Christian *osteotheke*, with thirty six secondary interments, was dug by Catling in 1974. The cemetery character of the area north of the city of Knossos in post-Minoan times was fully revealed in 1978 when the Medical Faculty site, an area of some five to six acres, was dug, under pressure, over a period of six months and occupied the Knossos Fellow, Jill Carington Smith, and many members of the School from Athens. Over three hundred interments were excavated, many in Chamber Tombs dating from the end of the Minoan period and re-used over and over again in Proto-geometric, Geometric, and Early Orientalising times; others were in pit-graves, especially of Hellenistic date, and there were some Roman burials. The only structure was an Early Christian aisled Church, with associated ossuaries. Other rescue operations performed at the request of the Archaeological Service, were occasioned by channels for water-supply in 1974, and for telephone cables in 1977.

(B) THE REST OF CRETE

One of the first effects of the liberation and independence of Crete was the assignment to the foreign Schools of areas for excavation by the High Commissioner, Prince George of Greece. The second was the formation of the Cretan Exploration Fund, to be administered jointly by Arthur Evans and the School (in the persons of Hogarth, Bosanquet and Myres). No time was lost in putting it to use; Hogarth proceeded from his work at Knossos to the clearance of the Dictaean Cave at Psychro, with its remarkable hoard of Minoan votives, and to Kato Zakro. Here he first investigated some (probably votive) pits from which were recovered Late Minoan pottery of high quality; next, he partly cleared a group of solidly built Late Minoan houses on the slopes north of the valley, the source of a notable collection of sealings, many with fantastic designs, and was preparing to dig in the valley itself when a dramatic storm and floods swept away his encampment and brought work to a close.

Bosanquet was more fortunate. The inland site of Praisos had been partially explored by Federico Halbherr, in 1884 and 1894; the published finds included a group of terracottas and an 'Eteocretan' inscription in Greek letters but a non-Greek language. The School's excavations were on a considerable scale over two seasons, 1901–2. All three acropolis hills were investigated; the finds were of several periods, the Neolithic to LMIII at the cave of Skales, two Late Minoan built tholos tombs (one circular in plan, the other rectangular) with signs of later cult, and an early Iron Age shaft grave. The temenos at which Halbherr had worked yielded an early altar, and cult buildings of fifth and early fourth-century date; votive offerings dating from the eighth to the fifth century included handsome archaic figurines, miniature bronze armour, and more Eteocretan inscriptions. A Hellenistic building with fine ashlar masonry may have been a public edifice. The famous archaic painted pinax was found in the circular tholos tomb, associated with Geometric pottery.

His second venture, at Palaikastro (Roussolakkos) on an eastward facing bay further to the North, was again on a large scale, and lasted from 1902–1905. The main effort here was devoted to the Minoan town site where, overlying buildings of earlier periods, a considerable area of the Late Minoan town was excavated; its houses were well constructed, arranged in blocks connected by paved and drained streets. Its most flourishing period was Late Minoan IB, which ended in wholesale destruction, but a number of very well-built houses belonged to a period of resettlement in Late Minoan III. A wealth of pottery and small finds was recovered from all periods. Outlying houses and Early to Middle Minoan ossuaries and Late Minoan larnax burials were explored at several points. Nearby at Magasá, Dawkins, who was in charge of the dig for the later seasons, excavated a Neolithic house and a cave; at Petsofa, to the south, John Myres explored a Middle Minoan Peak Sanctuary with notable votive figurines. Not the least important discovery was that of the classical sanctuary of Dictaean Zeus overlying the town site; almost nothing remained of its buildings, though interesting architectural terracotta revetments, archaic or later, were recovered; but the incomplete inscription containing the Hymn of the Kouretes — inscribed not earlier than 200 A.D. but dating from not later than 300 B. C. — is of major importance for students of Greek religion.

The site was by no means exhausted; in 1962 Hugh Sackett and Mervyn Popham returned to it with the object of completing the sequence established in the first excavations and extending this, if possible, to the end of the latest Minoan period. Their excavations, in an untouched area to the west, exposed a large Late Minoan IB house of some eighteen ground-floor rooms (with traces of an upper storey); its handsome finds included important pottery imported from Knossos. Partial re-occupation of the town in Late Minoan IIIA and abandonment in Late Minoan IIIB was confirmed. Late Minoan IIIC occupation was found on the rocky headland of Kastri, where, overlying evidence of settlement in Early Minoan I and III, a fairly extensive settlement, mostly along the seaward edge, prompted comparison with 'a hill-top village of the present day'. Its pottery suggested the arrival of new settlers, probably from elsewhere in Crete. At the request of the Archaeological Council the opportunity was taken to clean up and rehabilitate the part of the old excavated area which had been left exposed.

In 1983 an intensive study of the whole Palaikastro area was undertaken by L. Sackett and A. MacGillivray, with the assistance of a magnetometer survey, and balloon photography provided by Professor J. W. Myers. This revealed how very much greater an area had been occupied by the Minoan town, especially along the coast.

Air view of Palaikastro, 1984

Sites in the upland plain of Lasithi were extensively explored by the Pendleburys and Mercy Money-Coutts during the 1930s. In 1913, a short campaign by Dawkins at Plati had revealed the existence of sizeable Late Minoan I and II buildings, in the arrangement of which J. W. Graham sees a resemblance to the grouping of palace buildings round a central court. A square tholos tomb (of Cretan type but eccentric plan) was also explored. Pendlebury's sites ranged from the Neolithic at the cave of Trapeza, where offerings also continued through the Early and Middle Minoan periods, through the settlement of Kastellos, Middle Minoan I to III, to the Dark Age refugee settlement on the peak of Karphi. Here a large area, a third of the whole, was cleared; its most important discovery was a shrine, from which came the large terracotta figurines of goddesses with uplifted arms and various attributes adorning their headresses. He also explored a number of sites which he did not live to publish; some are mentioned by him in *BSA* 36 (1935/6). Others are summarised by L. Vance Watrous (who has done much independent work on Lasithi) in *BSA* 75 (1980).

In south-central Crete two adjacent sites have recently been investigated near Myrtos. The smaller, Phournou Korifi, was completely excavated in 1967–8 by Peter Warren and published as *Supplementary Volume* No. 7, in 1972. It proved to be a settlement occupied in two phases of Early Minoan II, which then came to a violent end, and was never re-occupied. It comprised some ninety rooms within a boundary wall — hardly a fortification — many of which had clearly been applied to industrial uses; traces of fulling, weaving and other textile processes, and potters' wheels were also found. Other areas had been in domestic use; one group of rooms was a shrine, in which was found the charming pot-goddess holding her pot-infant in her arms.

On a second height, nearer to the village and falling steeply to the sea, the site of Myrtos Pyrgos was explored by Gerald Cadogan from 1970 to 1975. There were six main periods; Pyrgos I was roughly contemporary with Phournou Korifi, and may have suffered destruction at the same time. Pyrgos II covered the later Early and first part of the Middle Minoan period, its most notable features being a fine paved road leading to a paved court and a roughly rectangular built tomb, which remained in use into Pyrgos III (covering the rest of the Middle Minoan period), from which the main buildings recovered were a large circular cistern and the base of a tower. Pyrgos IV was a flourishing Late Minoan town, with houses and a system of streets on the east, west and north slopes, and, on the summit, a large and elegantly appointed country house, aligned north-south with a paved court to its south. In it were found, besides important pottery and stone vases, a shrine whose contents included a Linear A tablet. The settlement was destroyed by fire at the end of Late Minoan IB. Pyrgos V was a Hellenistic shrine, dedicated to Aphrodite and Hermes. Pyrgos VI, not yet thoroughly studied, is a beacon tower of possibly Venetian date.

West of Knossos, the School has excavated, briefly, at the Kamares Cave (Dawkins and Laistner, 1913), at Early Minoan tomb sites in the Agiofarango

Valley, as part of a multi-disciplinary survey by four archaeologists, a geologist, a human and a physical geographer, and at Debla, in the foothills of the White Mountains overlooking the Khania plain. The Agiofarango survey was done in 1971 and 1972, and published by Keith Branigan and David Blackman in *BSA* 72 (1977) (the same scholars had published their survey of another area of Southern Crete in *BSA* 70 (1975)). The excavation of the Early Minoan tholos at A. Kyriaki was undertaken in 1972, in collaboration with K. Davaras of the Greek Archaeological Service, and published in *BSA* 77 (1982). Debla, a joint dig in 1971 by Peter Warren and Y. Tsedakis (then Epimelete for Western Crete), brought to light a small open settlement of three Early Minoan phases, 'a small agricultural community, possibly seasonal'. It was published in *BSA* 69 (1974).

The background to all these excavations has been continual survey work; Arthur Evans himself travelled and observed widely (as too did the other 'fathers' of Cretan archaeology like Halbherr and Hazzidakis). Before, during and after his time as Curator of Knossos, Pendlebury and his colleagues travelled from end to end of the island; Hutchinson too visited and noted Minoan sites whenever his curatorial duties permitted. After the war, Sinclair Hood, often accompanied at various times by his wife, Warren and Cadogan, made surveys of selected areas (published in the *Annual*), and was the moving spirit in the underwater survey of Cretan harbours undertaken with John Leatham and published in BSA 53/4 (1958–9). Working from the School, John Betts, Keith Branigan, Mark Cameron and Peter Warren — to name but a few — have published valuable synoptic studies of Minoan seals, weapons, frescoes and stone vases, while John Boardman's publication of the objects found in the Idaean Cave and his majestic volume on rings and seals are major contributions to the archaeology of Crete.

(C) MELOS

In Melos, the site of Phylakopi was chosen for excavation after other possibilities had been tested; a general survey of the island was concurrently undertaken by Duncan Mackenzie and David Hogarth. Digging began in 1896, under Cecil Harcourt Smith, and continued for four seasons under Hogarth (1898) and Duncan Mackenzie, who had been present throughout.

The superimposed remains of three cities were found, and below these traces of an earlier, though still Bronze Age, settlement. Phylakopi I spanned the transition from the Early to the Middle Cycladic period, producing coherent house-plans and quantities of pottery of various well-distinguished fabrics. Phylakopi II, a walled town, covered most of the middle Cycladic; from its more developed houses were recovered not only pottery in genuine Cycladic style and local fabric but imported Cretan wares and (as was later established) much Minyan ware from the mainland. This town ended in a wholesale destruction. Phylakopi III, though described as 'the old civilisation in a new phase of its development', showed in its early stages powerful Cretan influence in building, fresco and pottery, as well as many Cretan imports. In its third phase, however, both its pottery and its palace 'megaron' were of mainland type, and part of its fortifications was also of this phase.

The archaeology of the Cyclades was in its infancy: a number of objects had been published earlier by Bent, and the considerable excavations of Christos Tsountas, mostly of cemeteries, in Syros, Amorgos, Paros, Siphnos and other islands, published in 1898 and 1899, provided much comparative material. Much more had been learnt about the Bronze Age of the mainland since Schliemann's discoveries at Mycenae and Tiryns. Knowledge of the Minoan civilisation of Crete, however, was still mainly to come. In spite of this undoubted handicap, the work done at Phylakopi, described by Blegen as 'the first really serious effort to understand stratification, the first really good excavation in Greece', has stood the test of time.

Its publication was undertaken by an editorial committee, consisting of Bosanquet, Ernest Gardner and G. F. Hill, and the resultant volume, *Excavations at Phylakopi in Melos*, appeared as *JHS Supplement* No. 4 in 1904. By this time Mackenzie was able to make use of his experience as Evans' assistant at Knossos to include as his contribution a chapter on 'Aegeo-Cretan Relations'.

The site was by no means exhausted, and work had been intermitted specifically 'in order to enable the School to commence operations in Crete' — as Hogarth promptly did. In 1911 the value of another purely stratigraphic excavation in an area 'purposely left untouched with a view to its further investigation when time should have thrown more light on the vexed questions of early Aegean civilisation' decided Dawkins (with Droop and a small team) to conduct a two-months campaign. Its results (published in *BSA* 17 (1910)) lay especial emphasis on the external relationships of prehistoric Melos.

The revival of Cycladic studies at the School in Athens began perhaps with a survey of Late Cycladic sites by Kathleen Scholes (*BSA* 56 (1961)), but is particularly linked with the work of Colin Renfrew from 1967 onwards. After the publication (in 1972) of *The Emergence of Civilisation*, it was logical for him to seek the opportunity of further work at Phylakopi; from 1974–7, with the cooperation in the field of Sinclair Hood, four areas were explored, and the walls exposed in earlier campaigns were consolidated. In the region of the megaron, the existence of a building of comparable size during Late Minoan IB was established, and fresco fragments were recovered which brought into question the ascription of previously found frescoes to the second city. The fortification walls were securely dated to Late Helladic IIIB, but an earlier double circuit, dating to Late Minoan IA/B, was traced outside them on the south. A small shrine or pair of shrines adjoining the city wall to the west, with phases lasting from Late Helladic IIIA to the desertion of the site at the end of the Mycenaean period, produced a very important series of male and female figurines, probably of deities, and large wheel-made animals. The shrine has been published as *Supplementary Volume* No. 18. A team from the University of Southampton conducted a survey of the island's obsidian sources and a variety of studies relating to the ancient and modern environment; these were published in *Melos, an Island Polity* (edited by Colin Renfrew and Malcolm Wagstaff) in 1982.

(D) SPARTA AND LACONIA

In 1906, after fruitful excavations of prehistoric sites at Phylakopi in Melos and Palaikastro in Eastern Crete, the School turned to its first major classical site, Sparta. Digging began on the acropolis, where its fortifications were traced and the scanty remains of the shrine of Athena Chalkioikos were cleared and identified, but was soon concentrated on the low-lying site of the sanctuary of Artemis Orthia, on the right bank of the Eurotas. The work was initiated by Bosanquet, in his last months as Director, but carried on over four seasons by his successor, R. M. Dawkins, who also brought its publication to fruition in 1929. Most members of the School shared in the excavation, or in the topographical surveys of Laconia carried out before or in parallel with it. The site proved to be of the first importance; while its architecture was undistinguished — as at most Laconian sites — the wealth of dedications, especially the ivories, provided a totally new view of the elegance and richness of Archaic Spartan art, and the abundance of stratified pottery, in association with Corinthian fabrics, gave the first sure basis for a classification of the Laconian wares, and securely anchored 'Cyrenaic' painted vases to their true Spartan provenance. The peculiarly Spartan forms of offerings, lead figurines and clay masks, were found in profusion; both sculpture and inscriptions were recovered in quantity.

As a preliminary to the excavation, Tod and Wace prepared a catalogue of the existing collection in the Sparta Museum (published in 1906). From 1904, singly or in pairs, members of the School surveyed all districts of Laconia, noting sites and objects of all periods and occasionally conducting small excavations (Guy Dickins at Thalamai/Koutiphari; Wace and Hasluck at Geraki and Angelona). After reports of finds by shepherds at the Menelaion, high above the east bank of the Eurotas, two seasons digging established the existence east of the shrine building of extensive though ill-preserved Mycenaean houses. Four days digging, in 1910, at a site above the Kalyvia of Socha in the Taygetus foothills where floods had exposed lead votives, were enough to prove correct its identification, by earlier scholars, with the Eleusinion.

For some years the School's attention was directed elsewhere or to Bronze Age Studies, but when in 1923 a classical site was once more agreed to be desirable, both Wace and the Committee were anxious to resume work at Sparta, this time on the Acropolis and the theatre.

An appeal for funds was well supported, and in 1924, A. M. Woodward, once settled in as Director, began to dig on a fairly large scale. Only part of the huge theatre, Roman in date, was cleared; more of the Chalkioikos deposit, behind the

'Leonidas',
excavated at Sparta in 1927

cavea wall, was excavated, and some good bronzes recovered and worked on by
Winifred Lamb. There was a good crop of inscriptions, and one notable piece of
stone sculpture, the so-called Leonidas, recovered in 1925 from S. W. of the
Chalkioikos precinct. As on many Laconian sites, the most considerable remains of
buildings were of Roman or Byzantine date — a large Byzantine church was dug
on the eastern spur of the Acropolis — thus further illustrating Thucydides'
remarks about the unimpressive character of the Spartan capital.

One of the excavators was W. L. Cuttle who, after his return to Cambridge,
encouraged Robert Cook to take up the study of Laconian pottery. Payne decided
that the subject was better suited to Cook's co-student in Athens, Arthur Lane, who
accordingly took it over (Cook instead took up Fikellura), and his work came to
supersede the pioneer studies of Droop in *Artemis Orthia*. Wace was the moving
spirit behind the survey of Prehistoric Laconia (*BSA* 55 (1960) and 56 (1961),

Waterhouse and Hope Simpson), from which arose Lord William Taylour's decision to excavate at A. Stephanos in the Helos plain. The principal importance of this Bronze Age site, dug alternately with Mycenae between 1964 and 1975, was the finding, in quite considerable quantities, of Minoising pottery which bears a close resemblance to that found by Coldstream and Huxley at Kastri in Kythera.

British interest in Laconia was recognised in 1948 when small rescue excavations were undertaken, at the request of the Greek Ministry, at the Eleusinion and in an area south of the Sparta acropolis destined for a sports complex.

In 1973 Hector Catling returned with a considerable team to the Menelaion, with the object of dating the final destruction of the Mycenaean houses more closely, and in hopes of tracing other buildings between these and the Menelaion. Three large Mycenaean buildings, discontinuous in date, were uncovered, and, on an adjacent hill, the first Late Helladic IIIC settlement in the Eurotas valley. Fine inscribed bronzes found during cleaning round the shrine itself established beyond doubt its dedication to Menelaos and Helen. Sufficient traces of an earlier Menelaion were found to enable a paper reconstruction to be made in the long summary report in *Archaeological Reports for 1976/7*. Since the conclusion of the excavation, a survey of the area east of the Eurotas, from Sellasia to the Menelaion, has been put in hand.

The Menelaion and Taygetos, 1936

(E) MYCENAE

Schliemann's dazzling discoveries at Mycenae were followed by years of less spectacular but very important work by Greek archaeologists. Stamatakis excavated the Sixth Shaft Grave and four Middle Helladic graves in the Grave Circle, and cleared out the dromos of the Treasury of Atreus. In 1886 Christos Tsountas began six years of fruitful exploration, during which he found and/or cleared the rest of the nine tholos tombs and many rich and important Chamber tombs, and excavated most of the important features of the citadel, most notably the Mycenaean palace and the Greek temple which overlies it. In 1913 Keramopoullos made some investigations in the Grave Circle.

When the School was able to resume work in 1919, its selection of Mycenae was largely due to Sir Arthur Evans, who urged the importance of seeking permission to dig there 'in view of the great discoveries in Crete which have thrown entirely new light on the origin and development of the Mycenaean civilisation'. Wace was admirably equipped to undertake this as he had spent much of his spare time during the war in working on pottery from Mycenae in the National Museum, and had shared the American excavations of Carl Blegen at Korakou with whom, too, he had worked out and published the Helladic system of dating. Tsountas generously waived his rights on the site, and work began in April 1920, continuing annually thereafter until 1923. For the first two years Wace had the assistance of Blegen, as well as of many members of the School, and Leicester Holland, also of the American School, shared the duties of architect with Piet de Jong and contributed to the final report. The excavation programme was extensive; within the citadel, stratigraphic studies were carried out at the Lion Gate, the Grave Circle, the Great Ramp; the Granary by the Lion Gate was thoroughly investigated — Granary Style pottery being first identified here — good fresco remains were found below the Ramp House (and studied by Winifred Lamb), the area of the South House and the Hellenistic houses over it was started. All parts of the Palace were probed, studied and re-interpreted, and more important pieces of fresco brought to light. Outside the citadel, all the tholos tombs were restudied, though the complete clearance of the Tomb of Aegisthus, which had eluded Tsountas also, proved too hazardous for the Committee to sanction. The Mycenaean watchtower on A. Elias was cleared, and a whole cemetery of chamber tombs on the Kalkani Hill was excavated. These were published as *Archaeologia* 82 (1932); everything else, after comparatively brief reports in *BSA* 24 (1922), appeared with astonishing speed and completeness in *BSA* 25 (1923), surely the most weighty number ever published. Winifred Lamb shared in the account of the palace and undertook all the fresco studies. Walter Heurtley restudied all the stelai from the Grave Circle; Axel Boethius undertook the account of Hellenistic Mycenae. All the rest was written by Wace, in a masterly combination of meticulous detail and overall interpretation. Unfortunately the thrust of his conclusions, that the great period of the finest tholos tombs and of the acropolis was Late Helladic III, proved unacceptable to Evans and Myres, who devoted considerable scholarly energy and ingenuity to attempt to disprove them. This unhappy schism made it difficult for a number of years for Minoan and Mycenaean studies to be pursued as a whole and without partisanship, though both Pendlebury and Hutchinson, successive Curators of Knossos, had experience as 'Mycenaeans'.

When Wace was able to return to Mycenae in 1939 it was in the hope of demonstrating the validity of the earlier work. This was most successfully achieved by a series of probes behind the dromos walls and round the dome of the Treasury of Atreus, where evidence of every kind, especially thousands of Late Helladic II/III sherds in a deposit through which the dromos passage had been cut, not only dated the great monument even more firmly to Late Helladic III but threw much light on the methods of its construction. Tombs dug outside the citadel to the north-west bore out the view, first formulated by Tsountas, that before the city walls were built the Grave Circle was originally part of an old and extensive cemetery. Digging on the summit, below the temple terrace to the north, was crowned with the recovery of the famous ivory triad. Lower down, and east of the palace, the House of Columns (originally found by Tsountas) was cleared and planned afresh, and provided good comparative material for the interpretation of the house of Odysseus in the *Odyssey* (later work here by Mylonas enabled him to identify the whole complex as part of the palace itself).

The war made further digging impossible and severely curtailed the time available for studying the finds. A serious casualty of the war years was the loss of almost all the 1920–23 stratigraphic material, and the destruction and confusion of much of the 1939 pottery, when the basement in which it was stored, in the Nauplion Museum annexe, was used as an air-raid shelter. Wace was unable to resume work at Mycenae until 1950, though in 1949 he published *Mycenae, an archaeological History and Guide* which set out for the general reader the results of earlier work. In six campaigns, from 1950 to 1955, and with many helpers, he undertook a wide programme of excavation; within the Citadel, the House of the Warrior Vase (dug by Schliemann), and Tsountas' House were re-dug, and a new area, the Citadel House, begun; more of the Prehistoric Cemetery was dug, and an area north-west of the Lion Gate, noted but not more than 'scratched' in 1923, as the Cyclopean Terrace Building, was thoroughly explored and extended to reveal the earlier House of the Wine Merchant. More work was done on several of the Tholos tombs; a substantial poros wall east of the dome of 'Clytemnestra' afforded further confirmation that, as Stamatakis was the first to suggest and as was borne out by the 1939 results round 'Atreus', the mounds of earth over the domes of tholoi were kept in place by supporting walls. New ground was broken to the west of the citadel with the excavation of three important adjoining buildings, the Houses of the Oil Merchant, of Sphinxes, and of Shields, all of Late Helladic IIIB1 date. Their finds included not only some splendid ivories but the first group of inscribed Linear B tablets to be found at Mycenae. (Work on the House of Sphinxes and of the Oil Merchant was continued after Wace's death by his daughter Lisa French, in 1959 and 1961.) Knowledge of classical Mycenae was enlarged by the excavation and study of the Perseia Fountain House not far outside the Lion Gate, and, by John Cook, of the eighth-century sanctuary of Agamemnon by the Mycenaean bridge below the citadel.

After Wace's death, overall direction of excavations at Mycenae was resumed by the Greek Archaeological Society, first by Papadimitriou and, after his premature death, by Mylonas. In association with these, Lord William Taylour from 1960 resumed work on the Citadel House, in not quite consecutive campaigns until 1969. Besides much valuable new information about successive destructions at Mycenae in the thirteenth and twelfth centuries B.C. the most notable of his discoveries were (1968–9) of two, possibly three, shrines with which were associated an astonishing series of large terracotta idols, many of fearsome aspect, ivories of quality, and a remarkable fresco with the upper part of three goddesses or votaries.

Meanwhile, in a series of fundamental articles in the *Annual* from 1963 to 1969, Lisa French studied the successive phases of Late Helladic III pottery from Mycenae; supplementary studies by Ken Wardle and Penelope Mountjoy also appeared, dealing with the pottery from the Citadel House. The excavation reports by Wace and others, as published in the *Annual*, are now collected in *Supplementary Volume* No. 12; the results of the excavations between 1959 and 1969 are being embodied in 'Well-built Mycenae', a work of many hands under the overall editorship of Taylour, French and Wardle.

(F) PERACHORA

When Humfrey Payne proposed Perachora as the site for an excavation he did not expect this to last more than one season. The headland and its small harbour were remote and waterless, and little mentioned in ancient sources. The quantity, quality and importance of the finds, however, was such as to occupy him and his team for a full four seasons digging, from 1930 to 1933. The heart of his work was the valley above the harbour, site of the sanctuaries of Hera Akraia and Hera Limenia, with their temples and public buildings, including a sacred pool. Other areas more slightly explored were the upper valley, the 'town site', and the fortifications above the lighthouse. These latter areas, and the remarkable hydraulic works necessary for their population, were further explored by Dunbabin in 1939, and in 1964–6 under Megaw's direction by Tomlinson, J. J. Coulton, and E. J. A. Kenny, whose work was published in *BSA*.

Work began in 1930 with the sixth-century temple of Hera Akraia,, excavation of which was not completed until 1932. The earlier temple of Hera Limenia and the sacred pool below it, the harbour area with its stoa and the 'Agora' were also dug over this period. Excavation of the earliest temple of all, an apsidal structure originally dated to the middle of the ninth century, was made possible only in 1933,

Bronze Herakles from Perachora

when a chapel of St. John, which was built over its area, was removed to a new site. The votive deposits of all these shrines were of great richness in bronzes, ivories and pottery; of great importance were parts of terracotta models of an early temple, possibly reproducing the form of the actual (Geometric) shrine itself. The reader is referred to the two large volumes, *Perachora* I (1940) and II (1962).

The L-shaped stoa by the harbour, dug in 1932, is referred to only briefly by Payne in *Perachora* I. It was restudied and fully published by Coulton in *BSA* 69 (1964); he was able to date it to the end of the fourth century, but could offer no firm suggestion as to its function in the sanctuary.

West of the harbour and some four metres above it, the small enclosed area, called during its excavation in 1932, 1933 and 1939 the Agora but now re-named the West Court, was further explored in 1964 and 1966 (Megaw, Coulton and Tomlinson). In shape it was an irregular pentagon, about 24m 'square', with benches along the south, south-east and west walls. Along the west and south-west walls was an L-shaped portico, its roof supported on pillars. The walls are of different types and periods, polygonal on the east, the rest orthostatic. In its earliest phase the court was open on two sides and seems to have been merely an extension of the area round the temple, and constructed slightly later than it, some time in the sixth century. Its later enclosure suggests some specific function, but there is nothing to show what this might have been. Its final form has been dated by Coulton to after 350, and connected with other important new constructions of the late fourth century, the Stoa, the facade of the Fountain House, and perhaps the water shafts and the Hestiatorion (Dining-room).

Another group of monuments in the Heraion valley was the large double-apsidal roofed cistern and the Hestiatorion beside it to the south. These were excavated by Payne but are not described in *Perachora* I or II, so in 1964 Richard Tomlinson was asked to undertake their publication. A short season of clearing and excavation was undertaken in that year, and work continued in 1966 when Tomlinson also studied the large and complex waterworks on the Upper Plain; for these he had the assistance of Kenny, who had been in charge of this section of the original excavations in 1933. The cistern was of ashlar construction, with a central row of piers to support the roof (probably of planks). It was supplied from a branch of the great drain which carried off the rainfall from the valley's upper terraces; the water entered the cistern via a settling tank at its eastern end. Beside it and on the same orientation a building consisting of three rooms, a long anteroom and two square rooms with stone couches round their walls, was identified as a Hestiatorion, and dated, like the Stoa and Court, to the late fourth century; later work, however, has led him to date it early, to the late sixth or early fifth century. Humbler structures of similar plan in the upper plain were also identified as Hestiatoria, and connected, like this one, with the entertainment of selected guests from among those attending the festivals of Hera.

Another series of interconnected water installations in the upper valley (originally worked on by Kenny) was reinvestigated, and the functioning of its several parts explained. From three deep rectangular shafts reaching down to the water-table, which were approached by a long stairway and horizontal tunnels, water was raised by endless chains of buckets over large wheels set in the shafts; a system of poles and cogs connecting the wheels to a horizontal axle turned by oxen may have been intended, but was never installed. The wheels were probably turned by a treadmill. The water was fed into a lined channel which led to a set of three long cisterns, connected with three deep draw-basins. The roof was formed by the stratum of hard rock, which here forms a scarp. In front of the draw-basins, at a lower level, a fountain house was built, with an Ionic hexastyle prostyle façade. The whole system was again dated to the late fourth century, the period of re-development of the Heraion. It seems to have been designed to cope with heavy but intermittent demand for water, and to suggest that the scanty buildings in the upper plain were not, as had been thought, remains of a town, but rather — except for possibly two farms — to cope with festival crowds of visitors.

In 1982 Tomlinson returned to Perachora to investigate a large circular structure immediately above the Heraion valley, which was under threat from possible development. The structure, 28m in diameter, was of several courses of ashlar construction, and lined with waterproof cement. Presumably therefore it was another waterworks building, and the excellence of its masonry suggests a date in the fifth century. Tomlinson writes, 'There can be little doubt that this is the circular building in which (as Xenophon records) Agesilaos sat in 392'. Further work on this part of the site has been held up by uncertainties about the ownership of the land.

Further afield, a small cemetery of the sixth and early fifth centuries was dug in 1937 by Dunbabin at Monasteri.

(G) CHIOS

The School's interest in Chios is of long standing. Hasluck's study of the Latin Monuments of the island was published in *BSA* 16 (1910). Work on earlier antiquities began for the School when in April, 1934, Winifred Lamb re-opened excavations at the site of the temple of Apollo at Kato Phana in southern Chios in the hope of discovering more about the Archaic period of the island in particular. Kourouniotis had already made important finds in excavations here in 1913 immediately after the liberation of Chios from Turkish rule. Lamb's work was published in *BSA* 35 (1934/5).

In 1934 Edith Eccles made archaeological expeditions in Chios, and these were followed by a comprehensive survey of the Classical antiquities of the island by (Sir) David Hunt in 1938 (*BSA* 41 (1940/5)). The Genoese and later architecture was studied in the middle 1930s by Alexander Walton and Arnold Smith. The latter's work was published posthumously in 1962 as *The Architecture of Chios*.

In 1938 and 1939 Edith Eccles excavated in two important early prehistoric caves at Ayio Gala in the northwest corner of the island. The excavations here were largely financed by the late Dr Philip Argenti, who persuaded the School to embark upon work in Chios on a larger scale after the war with the object of obtaining further information about the early history of his native island. The work was entrusted to the general direction of Sinclair Hood, and began with excavations on the Kophina ridge on the northern edge of the ancient city of Chios in June, 1952. These were conducted by S. Hood, J. K. Anderson and R. V. Nicholls, and were published by J. K. Anderson in *BSA* 49 (1954).

In June 1952, S. Hood noted the existence of a prehistoric site at Emporio east of Kato Phana on the southern coast of Chios and made trials there. He also examined a Bronze Age cemetery and a late Roman built tomb in the region of Dotia near Emporio. Excavations were continued at Emporio from 1953–1955. The prehistoric site with deposits ranging from Neolithic to latest Mycenaean (Late Helladic IIIC) was further explored. A fortified late Roman settlement on the highest part of the prehistoric site and an Early Christian basilica church adjacent to it were also examined. These were largely excavated and recorded by M. Ballance and G. U. S. Corbett. John Boardman explored an early Greek sanctuary and apsidal temple on the site of the later basilica church, and an early

Greek city with fortified acropolis and temple of Athena on the hill of Profitis Ilias above Emporio. The Greek excavations were published by Boardman as *Supplementary Volume* No. 6 in 1967. The prehistoric excavations there and material from the excavations by Edith Eccles at Ayio Gala before the war were published by Hood in *Supplementary Volumes* Nos. 15 and 16 (1981, 1982).

In 1954 Boardman excavated a Classical farm house at Pindakas just inland from Emporio (*BSA* 53/4 (1958/59)). He also made soundings in the fortress built by the Athenians at Delphinion (near modern Langada) on the east coast north of the city of Chios when the island revolted during the Peloponnesian war (*BSA* 51 (1956)). The site had been identified by W. G. Forrest from air photographs in 1953.

In connection with the work at Emporio an under-water survey was made in June and July, 1954, round the south and east coasts of Chios by a party of divers using equipment (aqualungs and compressor) obtained through the generosity of Lord Kelmsley and the *Sunday Times* newspaper. Dilys Powell (formerly Mrs Humfry Payne) accompanied the expedition for part of the time as representative of the *Sunday Times*. The results were published by Richard Garnett and John Boardman in *BSA* 56 (1961).

The inscriptions of Chios have been exhaustively studied by W. G. Forrest in *BSA* 58 (1963), 59 (1964) and 61 (1966).

In the early 1970s a thorough topographical survey of the island was made by Eleftherios Yalouris (an American of Chiot descent) as part of the work for an Oxford doctoral thesis.

(H) OLD SMYRNA

From 1948 to 1951 the School's main site for excavation was at Bayraklı, a mound some 400m long — in antiquity perhaps largely a peninsula — to the north of the modern city of Izmir, itself roughly in the position of the New Smyrna founded in the time of Alexander the Great. This was a joint Anglo-Turkish project, directed on the Turkish side by Professor Ekrem Akurgal and for the School by its Director, John Cook, with James Brock as coadjutor for the first two seasons. A large team of students from the School took part; several remember with gratitude the efficient catering of Ursula Brock and Enid Cook.

The site proved to be a tell, with many successive layers of habitation, from the time of Troy I and, with a gap, through the second millennium B.C., to the abandonment of the site, on the orders of Alexander, in favour of the new foundation at the Pagos. Its largely peninsular character, normal for early settlements, seems well established, though it is now some way from the sea. The most flourishing period was that of Archaic Smyrna, which was destroyed, evidently by the Lydian King Alyattes, about 600 B.C. The excavation included part of his gigantic siege mound at the north end, thrown up to surmount the city wall.

Ivory lion from old Smyrna

Of great importance was the investigation by R. V. Nicholls, executed and published with exemplary speed and diligence, of a succession of city walls; that of the time before the Lydian sack was the most imposing, with a thickness, in one place, of some fifteen metres at its base. This was published, with a large site plan, in *BSA* 53/4 (1958/9), with a general study of the site and some classes of pottery.

A highlight of the excavation was the discovery of the Archaic temple, dedicated to Athena. Notable were its entrance passage, with a pylon and a stepped incline leading up to the temple platform; its exceptionally fine ashlar and polygonal masonry was preserved to a height of two to three metres. At the time of the sack a new and much larger temple was under construction; capitals of a new lotus-and-leaf type and some column drums from this were recovered. The finds from the temple area included faience and metal objects, Early Corinthian perfume flasks, figurines of ivory and terracotta, and votive spear- and arrow-heads. Professor Akurgal resumed excavations here in 1966 which have continued.

Houses were revealed all over the site. Those of the late eighth century were mainly curved or oval in plan; after their destruction, probably by earthquake, about 700 B.C., they were succeeded by commodious rectangular buildings, some of fine masonry (preserved in places up to a metre), others of mud-brick on high stone footings. A sixth-century housing complex with equally well-preserved walls, and three superimposed levels of fourth-century housing also came to light. Like the temple, these have been published by Akurgal in *Alt Smyrna I: Wohnschichten und Athenatempel* (1983). Further studies of both by Cook and Nicholls are in preparation.

Finds of pottery were everywhere abundant — in the final season a Festival of the Millionth Sherd was celebrated — ranging from Protogeometric through Geometric, Orientalising (both East Greek and Corinthian), East Greek black-figure and Attic black- and red-figure. Domestic wares and objects included bath-tubs, cooking pots, braziers and baking-trays, pithoi and wine amphorae. The material is still under study; with the fixed points provided by the sack by Alyattes and an apparent abandonment of the site in the 490s at the time of the Ionian revolt against the Persians, and with the frequent correlations with well-dated Corinthian and Attic wares, this will add greatly to knowledge of the development of East Greek pottery and to the cultural history of Ionia. A necropolis to the north-east of the city belonged largely to the period before 490; painted Clazomenian sarcophagi found here and elsewhere at Bayraklı are published by R. M. Cook in *BSA* 69 (1974).

Great historical importance must be attached to the information given by this excavation about the growth of an East Greek city. From the ill-constructed huts of the eighth century the citizens progressed to spacious homes of fine masonry, with several rooms, laid out on a regular north-south axis; from occupying part of a restricted peninsula, during the seventh century they extended their habitation to the mountain foot to the North and across the bay to the east. Other reports on the British work at the site have appeared in *BSA* 59 (1964) and 60 (1965).

(1) LEFKANDI

The full importance of this site only became clear as its excavation proceeded. Selected initially from indications on the surface that it might elucidate problems of Euboean history from the Dark Age down, at least, to the period of Euboean colonisation and the Lelantine War, Xeropolis has provided a totally new appreciation of the extent and complexity of Protogeometric civilisation; in addition, its earlier levels revealed a hitherto unsuspected late Early Bronze Age culture with strong Anatolian features, and a very important succession of habitation periods of the last century or so of the Bronze Age.

The settlement lies on an eroded hill on the coast about half-way between Chalkis and Eretria. The first three excavation seasons, 1964–1966, were more-or-less confined to this area; later work, in 1969–71 and from 1981 to the time of writing, was largely concentrated on the five cemeteries 600m inland to the north, the 147 graves and 80 pyres of which were found to date almost wholly to the late- and sub-Protogeometric periods. Their contents, which included a surprisingly large amount of gold jewellery and objects of faience, revealed not only a level of

The site at Lefkandi (photo, Mervyn Popham)

prosperity hitherto unexpected at this period, but a wide range of foreign contacts, notably with Egypt. They also demonstrated the independent ceramic development of Euboea, in spite of its closeness to, and established contacts with, Athens, generally regarded as the origin and inspiration of all Protogeometric styles. Another surprise find was a fine terracotta centaur. The most surprising and spectacular discovery of all, however, to which the excavations since 1980 have been devoted, was that of a large apsidal Heroon, containing a double shaft-grave; from one half was recovered the cremation burial of a warrior, whose bones, contained in a bronze figured krater, were wrapped in a cloth tunic — the first textile ever to be recovered, and restored, from this period; beside the urn lay sword and spear, and in parallel with it an extended female inhumation burial with rich gifts. The other half of the shaft contained the skeletons of four horses. Everything about this part of the Toumba cemetery was new; the size, 45 by 10 metres, of the Heroon building, and its peripteral character; its almost immediate abandonment (which seems certain), possibly even before its completion, and its covering over with a mound of unburnt brick; the evidence of the exalted status of the warrior buried in it, and the nature of the grave gifts; the horse sacrifice, unparalleled between the Late Bronze Age and the rich seventh-century tombs of Cypriot Salamis; and finally the closeness with which other graves, presumably of the same family, clustered round the Heroon.

Erosion had removed all but traces of what must have been a large Proto-geometric settlement on Xeropolis. One apsidal house plan was recovered, the life of which extended into the Geometric period, after which the settlement seems to have been abandoned. Filling material, apparently brought in from elsewhere on the site, contained pieces of clay moulds for casting tripod legs, to be dated about 900 B.C.

The Bronze age material, though of secondary importance, and from a smaller area, being confined to parts of Xeropolis itself, had much of significance. Its first phase, in a late stage of the Early Bronze Age, produced pottery with marked Anatolian characteristics, quite unlike contemporary Early Helladic III wares, but now paralleled by similar wares from nearby Manika and from Kastri in Syros. Thereafter the normal Middle and Late Bronze Age sequence was present until a

*Clay centaur
from the Lefkandi cemetery*

destruction in Late Helladic IIIB. Of great importance was a stratified Late Helladic IIIC sequence, initiated apparently by newcomers; its second phase produced a wide range of pictorial motives.

The excavations, begun for the School by L. Sackett and M. R. Popham and carried out with the assistance of many members of the school, have since 1981 been a joint operation with the Greek Archaeological Service and its Euboean Ephorate, represented in 1981 by E. Touloupa and subsequently by P. Kalligas.

(J) CYPRUS

Soon after the foundation of the School, the Cyprus Exploration Fund was opened to finance excavations in the Island, since 1878 a British-administered Turkish territory. It was hoped to introduce some order in a field where chaos reigned through indiscrimate pillaging of ancient sites. The Fund's operations were placed under the control of the Director of the School.

The sanctuary of Aphrodite at Old Paphos (Palaeopaphos) was chosen for the first excavation in 1888, conducted by E.A. Gardner, the Director, D. G. Hogarth and M. R. James and published in *JHS* 9 (1888). The almost complete denudation of the site which they found was a disappointment, but the large number of Greek inscriptions recovered was some compensation and the plan made of the surviving remains (by R. Elsey Smith) provided a basis for all later investigations.

The next year, Gardner, drawn by reported finds of Attic vases, opened a season of exploration in the cemeteries at Polis tis Chrysochou (Marion- Arsinoe), which J. A. R. Munro and H. A. Tubbs continued and published in *JHS* 11 (1890). It met with only moderate results, apart from a notable series of syllabic inscriptions.

In 1890 the same team conducted extensive explorations at Salamis, which established the topography of the site (*JHS* 12 (1891)). They identified the long Agora with its temple mound at one end and a great Byzantine cistern at the other, and excavated much of the marble peristyle later identified as the palaestra of the gymnasium. By trenching elsewhere they also set the scene for later excavators: at 'The Drums' (basilica of St Epiphanius), the 'Campanopetra' (another great basilica) and the 'Oil-press' installed, as the French Mission established, on re-occupation of an abandoned mansion of the fifth-century A.D. With marble sculpture from the peristyle, numerous Greek inscriptions and the spectacular bull's head capital now in the British Museum, the excavators could modestly claim 'a fair measure of success'.

J. L. Myres, a student of the School since 1892, was two years later assigned the balance of the Cyprus Exploration Fund, which he applied to a series of small excavations in cemeteries at Nicosia (Ayia Paraskevi) and Kalopsida, covering the Early and Middle Bronze Age, and at Larnaca (Turabi Tekke), where tomb groups ranging from the Geometric to the Roman period were found (*JHS* 17 (1897)). These controlled excavations materially assisted in establishing a chronology for the re-organisation of the initial collections of the Cyprus Museum, which he undertook the same year. This led to Myres' publication in 1899, with the help of Ohnefalsch-Richter, of the *Handbook of the Cyprus Museum*, the first systematic conspectus of the archaeology of the Island.

In the meantime, the British Museum had taken the lead by conducting excavations at Amathus in 1894, when Myres superintended work in both the east and west cemeteries; also at Curium (1895), Enkomi (1896) and Maroni (1897), where tombs rich in Mycenaean vases were found. But, by the turn of the century, rival attractions in Egypt and Crete had turned attention away from Cyprus.

In 1913 Myres, by then Wykeham Professor of Ancient History at Oxford and a member of the Managing Committee of the School, undertook excavations for the Committee of the Cyprus Museum designed *inter alia* to familiarise his pupil Menelaos Markides, lately appointed Curator, with the techniques of field archaeology (*BSA* 41 1940/5)). In addition to trials on the city sites of Citium (Bamboula) and Lapethus (Lamousa), the first tombs were dug in the Early Bronze Age cemetery to the west of the latter. At Enkomi, where no tombs could be dug owing to the high water table, Myres was the first to observe that the house-walls overlying them had survived from the related Bronze Age settlement, whose impressive remains were later to be uncovered.

Between the wars the excavations of Gjerstad's Swedish expedition and of Porphyrios Dikaios (Curator of the Cyprus Museum and a student of the School) carried the prehistory of the Island back to the Neolithic, and the School encouraged work in the early periods by sponsoring excavations in the spectacularly productive Early Bronze Age cemetery at Vounous-Bellapais by James Stewart of Sydney, who had come to the School by way of Cambridge in 1935/6.

More recently, the School has supported the resumption by Peter Megaw of the only large-scale excavation so far on a Medieval site, Saranda Kolonnes at Paphos, where the uncovering of a Crusader castle overlying earlier remains was completed in 1984.

(K) NORTH AFRICA

Apart from Old Smyrna and Cyprus, the School has found itself actively involved in excavation elsewhere outside the country of Greece — in North Africa. In 1884/5 the distinguished Egyptologist W. M. F. Petrie explored the ruins of the site at Naucratis in the Nile Delta. It was an Egyptian town to which had been added a Greek trading post, in the later part of the seventh century B.C. It was long to be the major Greek settlement in Egypt, though not a real 'colony', and its archaeological value lay not only in the rich finds of Greek material from its early years but in the light it shed on relations between Greece and Egypt in the Archaic period. It naturally excited the attention of Hellenists and the second season there

*Hogarth's
excavations
at Naucratis, 1899*

(1885/6) was conducted for the Egypt Exploration Fund by Ernest Gardner, later Director of the School at Athens. This led to direct School interest in the excavations which were continued by Hogarth and completed in 1903, with the results published in *BSA* 5 (1898/9) and *JHS* 25 (1905). The finds, especially of Archaic Greek pottery of high quality, came mainly to the British Museum but were also liberally distributed elsewhere, a fact that has militated against their complete publication, but the early reports demonstrated their importance to the world of scholarship and it may well be that the subsequent British record in study of Archaic pottery owes much to the School's part in this excavation in Egypt. And if this is true, it in part accounts for the School's second adventure on African soil eighty years later.

In 1963 the British archaeologist Richard Goodchild was Director of Antiquities in Cyrenaica (Kingdom of Libya) busily exploring the rich Roman cities of the coast. At Tocra (ancient Teucheira) a chance find of complete Archaic Greek vases on the shore led him to appeal to the British School at Athens for help and, as a first measure, John Hayes went to Libya to make a preliminary study of the finds. This was followed in 1964–5 by three seasons of excavation led by John Boardman, which uncovered, in a small but remarkably productive area on the beach at Tocra, well stratified deposits of votive pottery from a sanctuary of Demeter and Kore, which must have been founded by the first Greek settlers there, in the 620's B.C. Most of the finds were of the late seventh and sixth centuries, the richest single assemblage of its type and date from North Africa, after Naucratis. The excavations were published in *Supplementary Volumes* Nos. 4 and 10 (1966, 1974), with the second of which the School was happy to associate the newly founded Society for Libyan Studies, which continued work on remains of other periods on the site.

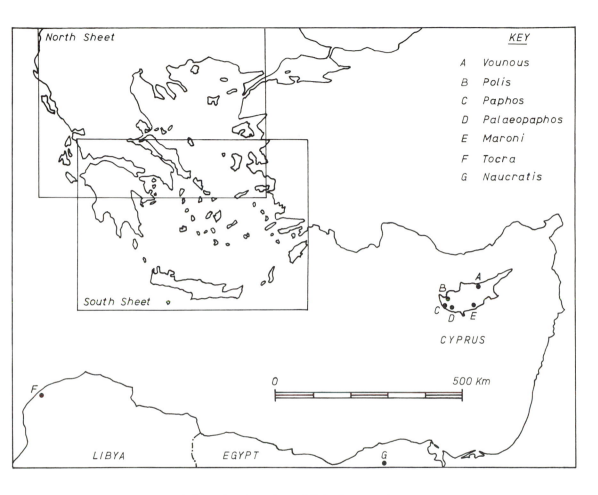

Maps showing sites of School excavations.

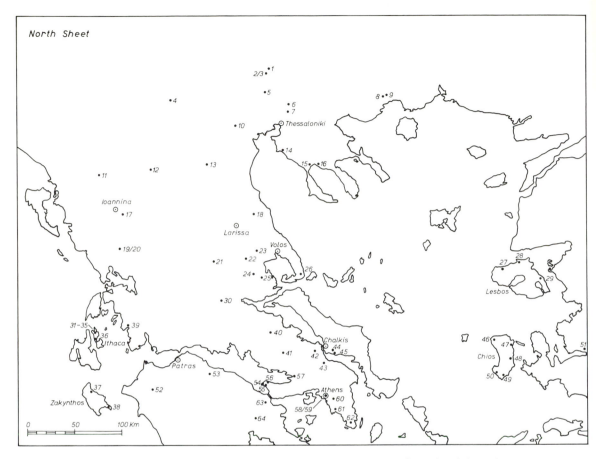

North Sheet

Scale: 0   50   100 Km

KEY TO MAPS

1	Kilindir
2	Chauchitsa
3	Vardina
4	Armenochori
5	Vardaroftsa
6	Assiros Toumba
7	Saratse
8	Mt. Pangaeus Cave
9	Sitagroi
10	Nea Nikomedeia
11	Klithi
12	Boubousti
13	Servia
14	Kritsana
15	Ayios Mamas
16	Molyvopyrgo
17	Kastritsa
18	Rachmani
19	Asprokhaliko
20	Kokkinopilos
21	Tsani
22	Tsangli
23	Pherae
24	Zerelia
25	Halos
26	Theotokou
27	Antissa
28	Methymna
29	Thermi
30	Lianokladi
31	Pelikata
32	Polis
33	Stavros
34	Tris Langadas
35	Ay. Athanasios
36	Aetos
37	Akroterion
38	Kalogeros
39	Astakos
40	Abae
41	Haliartos
42	Rhitsona
43	Schimatari
*44	Lefkandi Cemetery
45	Lefkandi Settlement
46	Ayio Gala
47	Delphinion
48	Kophina Ridge
49	Emporio
50	Kato Phana
51	Old Symrna
52	Peneios Barrage Rescue

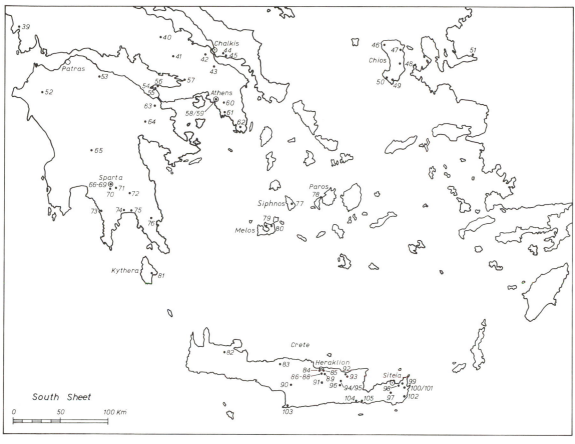

*39

*40
*41   Chalkis
          *44
*42   *45
          43
Patras
*53   *57
*52   *54 *56
      *55
  *63   Athens
              *60
  *64   *61
              *62

*65

        Sparta
66-69   *71
      *70
        *72
  *73 *74 *75
          *76

Kythera *81

46
Chios 47
        48
    50 49
51

Paros
*78
Siphnos *77

79
Melos *80

South Sheet

Crete
*82
      *83
          Heraklion
          84   92
86-88 85 93
      90 91 89 94/95
          96
              Siteia 99
              98 100/101
              97 102
      104 105
103

0   50   100 Km

KEY TO MAPS

53	Mamousia
54	Perachora Heraion
55	Vouliagmeni
56	Monasteri
57	Aegosthena
58	Olympieion
59	Kynosarges
60	Hymettus
61	Vari
62	Agrileza
63	Isthmia
64	Mycenae
65	Megalopolis
66	Sparta Acropolis
67	Artemis Orthia, Sparta
68	Great Altar, Sparta
69	Theatre
70	Kalyvia Sochas
71	Menelaion
72	Geraki
73	Thalamai
74	Ayios Stephanos
75	Asteri
76	Angelona
77	Siphnos Kastro
78	Antiparos Saliagos
79	Melos City
80	Phylakopi
81	Kythera Kastri
*82	Debla
83	Eleutherna
84	Fortetsa
85	Kephala Tholos
86	Knossos
87	Mavro Spelio
88	Villa Dionysus
89	Ailias
90	Kamares Cave
91	Gypsades
92	Karphi
93	Trapeza
94	Plati
95	Lasithi
96	Dictaean Cave
97	Praisos
98	Petras
99	Magasa
100	Palaikastro
101	Petsofa
102	Zakro
103	Ayia Kyriaki
104	Myrtos Pyrgos
105	Phournou Korifi

NOTE: * denotes joint Greek Archaeological Service/BSA excavation.

Chapter V

Other work of students

The founders saw the role of the School as the extension, the illumination, of classical scholarship. This is the abiding core of its students' work, the essential qualification for its Directors, the common interest of its oldest and most constant supporters. In a very few years after the foundation, Byzantine civilisation was added to classical; in a few more, the horizon extended backwards to the Bronze Age and the Neolithic. Then the living Greece, not its past only, its folklore, its social structure, became the object of scholarly (as well as affectionate) attention; no doubt the acquisitition of the Finlay Library provided some impetus in this direction. Studies were not confined to Greece proper, but from the beginning extended to Cyprus, the Levant and Asia Minor, and, more rarely, to Egypt and Cyrenaica.

The continuity of subject imposed on the other Schools by their commitment to 'permanent' sites, like Corinth, Delphi, Olympia or Phaistos, had no British School parallel until Evans' gift of Knossos. Sparta and Laconia have figured largely in the School's work, but there has never been a British-owned dig-house in Laconia. This absence of prior commitment has thrown School students much more on their own initiative in choosing their field of work, and circumscribed them less in the pursuit of it. In sessions when there was no large-scale School dig students, any time after February, could be found from Macedonia to Crete, Turkey to Albania, gathering material from the Neolithic to the Genoese, or simply seeing as much of Greece and its archaeology as possible. They travelled most frugally, usually uncomfortably, but difficulties, hazards or discomfort were not admitted as deterrents even by the earliest women students — Gisela Richter's enterprise was specially noted. Kitto strode the land from Tainaron to the equivalent of John O'Groats and, before Athens engulfed the School, lesser men and women could step out for daily exercise, almost from the Hostel gate, into unspoiled Attic countryside.

For some students, at all periods, the seeing was enough; if they had only one session in Greece there was no pressure, in early days at least, to produce some written evidence of their enlarged experience. Those who stayed longer almost always found, if they had not arrived with one, some field in which their work could become an addition to knowledge. Often there was an element of serendipity: Wace diverted from the Hellenistic to prehistory by 'falling in love' with Neolithic pottery, Romilly Jenkins diverted from Daedalic sculpture to Byzantine studies,

Vincent Desborough from the Trojan War to his fundamental studies of Proto-geometric, or Pendlebury's absorption in Cretan archaeology. In other cases the need to deal with objects turned up in excavations led to special studies in unforeseen directions (the Ithaca tripods, the Vari 'beehives') reaching beyond their original context.

Many students of course, notably epigraphists, arrived with their subjects clear in their minds; others were directed by their University teachers to definite topics. Some arrived with an unwillingness to look beyond or outside their chosen period or field of study, but few indeed found the single eye easy to preserve, and were the richer for their conversion.

Formal instruction has not played a large part in the life of the School. Bosanquet formulated, and *BSA* for many years printed, suggestions for intending students. These are reproduced in Appendix II, partly to illustrate the overwhelming importance of German scholarship at the time. It was required of Directors in the early days. Hogarth needed a special dispensation from the Committee to delegate lecturing to an Assistant Director, Professor G. C. Richards, to whom he relinquished part of his salary. After the first war Wace, Woodward and Payne are all on record as lecturing, in the Museums of Athens, on their special subjects. Students attended the lectures of Greek Professors and of other foreign Schools, and occasionally were conducted round their sites — Eleusis, the Agora, the Kerameikos — or were welcomed on their expeditions. Formal Open Meetings were held at the School each spring, at which resident or visiting scholars spoke to large audiences of Athenians. School expeditions, organised perhaps by Assistant Director or senior students, though not necessarily educational in intent, were very often so in fact. All this, though written in the past tense, is roughly the practice still prevailing at the time of writing. Informal seminars, initiated by Peter Warren when Assistant Director, have been held regularly from November to May, and act as a unifying factor in the face of the very large numbers of students and the great diversity of their subjects.

In the early years students came mainly from Oxford or Cambridge, where various funds, like the Craven and the Thomas Whitcombe Green, and graduate studentships already existed, and colleges also had scholarships for graduates. The 'School Studentship', founded in the earliest years, was offered in alternate years to the Vice-Chancellors of these universities for them to select suitable holders (the trouble this caused when the first woman holder was selected at Cambridge is dealt with below). Other English, Scottish and Irish universities sent some students, and from the 1890s women students attended, though they did not live in, the School. After the second war Dick Nicholls made history by being the first School Student from a Commonwealth University (Auckland); holders may now come from any university in the United Kingdom and Eire, and the emoluments are flexibly applied according to need and the existence or not of other funding. Named studentships specifically for work in Greek lands became more numerous over the years, at Oxford, Cambridge, Edinburgh, Dublin and many other universities, as the study of Greek archaeology came to be more widely taught — this to no small degree the effect of work done at the School and the dispersion of former students to academic positions.

In 1912 the Sachs Studentship was founded by his widow in memory of Gustav Sachs, who died in Athens in that year. It is given as funds permit and carries various conditions as to residence; the first holder was Lilian Chandler from Sheffield University. In 1928 George Macmillan founded the two-year Studentship which bore his name, to 'provide a revival of the type of "long-period" student who did so much for the welfare of the School before 1914 — a type which has become all too scarce, owing to changed conditions, in the last ten years'.

There had been architectural students at the School from the early days; many worked on the school's excavations, several also for Evans at Knossos. In 1929 the Royal Institute of British Architects founded its Athens Bursary, to be awarded to a member of the teaching staff of a School of Architecture recognised by the R.I.B.A., which brought more senior students to the School (it was accompanied by a welcome subscription of an annual £50 and the presence of an R.I.B.A. representative on the Committee).

Since 1948 D.E.S. (and now, British Academy) grants for graduate work have enabled more students to work in Athens. Partly as a corollary of this support, more of the students work for doctoral degrees; although no doubt intended as a spur to achievement if not a path to employment, this tends to make cross-fertilisation among students more difficult. One more source of student funding came in 1966 when the Greek Government offered ten scholarships a year to graduates from European countries for research in the Humanities; these are additional to the four scholarships offered annually by the Greek Ministry of Education through the British Council which, being available for a wide range of study, are seldom held at the School.

Students from the Commonwealth, always welcome, have recently increased in numbers, especially from Australia, and come from more places. The School numbers with pride among its old students Porphyrios Dikaios and Vassos Karageorghis, great Cypriot scholars and lasting friends; Sinclair Hood recalls that at the height of anti-British feeling in Greece over affairs in Cyprus Dikaios chose to stay in the School. Foreign students also have not been rare; after the first war the Norwegian, Swedish, Danish and Dutch archaeologists, who had before normally been given hospitality at the German Institute, were encouraged to attend the School; a party from Uppsala were admitted in 1919, the Dutch scholars, Dr and Mrs Hondius, lived in the School and worked at Mycenae, and C. A Boethius helped in its publication. Before the Swedish Institute in Athens was founded, in 1948 and thereafter until it had accommodation for students, parties of Swedes came often. It was as a student at the School that Emil Kunze reactivated the German Institute in 1950. In 1954/5 Danish students helped at the excavations in Chios. In recent years Japanese, Belgium, Polish and Yugoslav students have widened the School's intake.

It is impossible within reasonable compass to give a satisfactory account of the range of subjects treated by School members, and it would be hopelessly invidious to try to assess their value to scholarship. It is not enough to refer to the volumes of the *Annual*, although it has a prior claim to publish the work of students. Many pieces of work outgrow periodicals to become books — including the *Supplementary Volumes* — others remain unpublished but, as theses, are available in certain libraries.

Strictly archaeological studies range in time from the Palaeolithic of the mainland (first surveyed by Higgs), the Neolithic of Crete, the mainland and the islands, the Bronze Age — a heavy concentration here embracing site and area surveys, close studies of tombs, pottery, figurines, seals, bronzes, frescoes — to the Dark Ages. The growth and flowering of Greek culture from its beginnings has been studied in every aspect from the solid witness of inscriptions, the definition of pottery styles (most notably in orientalising fabrics), the evaluation and classification of sculptures, bronzes, coins and ivories, the history and reconstruction of architecture of all kinds, from temples and theatres to the country houses of Attica and the cisterns of Perachora. Many ancient historians began their graduate lives at the School, and their work is distinguished by its full use — in contrast with many volumes of the old style of history-writing — of archaeological evidence; the names of A. W. Gomme, H. T. Wade-Gery, N. G. L. Hammond, W. G. Forrest and D. M. Lewis, chosen at random, will stand for many others.

From the days of Weir-Schulz and Barnsley and the splendid publication of Osios Loukas, Byzantine studies have been at home in the School. In 1907/8 it was officially involved with the Byzantine Research and Publications Fund, and later absorbed it. Besides the monograph on the Great Church in Paros (Jewel and Hasluck), and much work on church architecture and decoration (Walter George, Traquair, Megaw), new ground was broken, from 1912 onwards, by the series of articles by H. J. W. Tillyard on Byzantine music. Later monuments studied include Crusader castles (Megaw, David Wallace and Karin Skawrin) and the Genoese and later architecture of Chios (Hasluck, Sandy Walton and Arnold Smith). Modern Greek literature has also received attention, notably by Romilly Jenkins and Philip Sherrard. Dialects and folklore were much studied in the early part of the century, Dawkins and Hasluck being particularly concerned with these matters. An article on Macedonian customs, by H. Triantaphyllides, appeared in *BSA* 3 (1896–7), showing how early the School recognised the value of such subjects. Hasluck's early death prevented him from emulating Dawkins' lifelong interest and achievement in this sphere, which also formed the life work, in Albania, of Margaret Hasluck. An anthropological approach has been prominent in the work of many recent students, taking up again studies like those of Wace on the Koutsovlachs and the Sarakatsani — the subject, indeed, of John Campbell, the 1984 Visiting Fellow. In that same year the Assistant Director, Roger Just, was a social anthropologist, and among Greek Government scholars were workers on geological surveys (Stymphalos), folk-art and embroideries, ornithology, agricultural co-operatives in Macedonia, and the entry of Greece into the EEC. As geology has been mentioned, this may be the place to refer to the very important work in Crete of Michael Durkin and his wife Carol Lister on quarries of all periods at Knossos and elsewhere (*BSA* 78 (1983)). Physical anthropology found a place at the School primarily for the study of bones found in excavations, for example recent work by Sheila Wall on the bones from the School's digs at Knossos. W. L. Duckworth who worked at Palaikastro, and also studied the cranial measurements of modern Cretans, made a special place for himself in the life of the region; he was regarded (according to the recollections of Tod) as almost a saint, and people came from miles around, at night, to the excavation house with implicit faith in his abilities to cure — he had in fact saved one man's sight by an operation.

Topography has occupied a special place in the work of the School, from the inauguration, by Cecil Smith, of the proposed 'dictionary of places, buildings, etc; with a complete list of references. . . grouped according to localities', and the topographical card index. It was as a student of the School that (Sir) James Frazer made the many journeys necessary for his *Commentary on Pausanias* — as also that author's more recent translator Peter Levi. In connection with excavations, surveys were made by Walter Loring (routes to Megalopolis), in Melos, in Laconia, and in Thessaly by Wace and Thompson. Between the wars came Heurtley's extensive work in Macedonia and his survey of prehistoric sites in Boeotia, Sylvia Benton's travels in the Ionian islands, and David Hunt's work in Chios, and later, Hood's; Nicolas Hammond and Robert Beaumont covered large tracts of Epirus, and a second, prehistoric, survey of Laconia was begun. This was completed, after the war, by Richard Hope Simpson, who went on to compile the valuable *Gazetteer of Mycenaean Sites* (1965), which was updated, with the collaboration of Oliver Dickinson, in 1979. The second edition, of wider geographical scope, included his work with John Lazenby in the Dodecanese; in both editions the Messenia section was due to the joint Hope Simpson-Macdonald site surveys published in the *American Journal of Archaeology*. The Cycladic Bronze Age was covered by Colin Renfrew but not published in topographical format. Jock Anderson collected classical sites in Achaea, Roger Howell prehistoric in Arcadia, and a large team combined in the Euboea survey. Unpublished theses containing Bronze Age surveys include Thessaly (Alan Hunter), sites west of Pindus (Ken Wardle) and a massive account of material from all over northern Greece by David French (later Director of the British School in Ankara). Overseas, John Cook, with G. E. Bean, surveyed the Greek sites of Anatolia — a by-product of the Smyrna dig; he also worked on the Troad, an area on which valuable work had been done many years before by Walter Leaf, one of the School's founders and first Honorary Treasurer.

In Crete, from the days of Sir Arthur Evans, British archaeologists have walked and ridden from end to end of the island, noting sites, routes, ports. John and Hilda Pendlebury, with Mercy Money-Coutts and Edith Eccles in the 1930s, were followed after the war by the Hoods, Warren and Cadogan, and Blackman and Branigan in Western Crete.

In recent years a more intensive kind of survey has come to the fore, which involves teams of walkers, in close formation, covering comparatively small areas at a time. In this way few surface indications are missed, and finds of all periods are recorded, though it may not be possible to be precise about the character of each. Several of these are mentioned above, but their results are not yet fully evaluated. Much is hoped from the use of scientific aids, such as the magnetometer recently employed at Palaikastro.

All admitted to the School in Athens are students, whether newly graduated or professors *emeriti*. The number who manage to stay for several sessions or who return during sabbaticals or long vacations would have delighted those who, like Bosanquet and Macmillan, were anxious to secure for the British School the benefits of continuity which they observed at the French School and German Institute. These professionals, whether or not they have been or later become officers of the School, edit the *Annual*, or sit on the Managing Committee, are and always have been the backbone of the School, its reservoir of expertise, goodwill and good advice, and their presence in it a source of pleasure and profit to students of all ages. In the early days they were polymaths, writing with equal authority on inscriptions or pottery, coins or the Bronze Age. With the remorseless growth of knowledge, and the enormous and expanding mass of material and of specialist literature, this universal competence has become unattainable. The application of scientific methods and techniques to archaeology, more than ever now, since the foundation of the Fitch Laboratory, an integral and very active part of the School's activities, adds another large branch to the tree of specialisation.

It must be confessed that those of an earlier generation sometimes open a newly-arrived book or periodical with apprehension. Will the rigors of presentation, the models and histograms of modern scientific archaeology, set a barrier between the reader and the desired knowledge to be found in its pages? Can it — for instance like the *Palace of Minos* — be read for pleasure by the writer's contemporaries? Perhaps this is but a recurrent phenomenon in the history of scholarship. In his address to the 1910 Annual Meeting the admirable Cecil Harcourt Smith appealed to members of the School to 'unbend a little', to make their work attractive to the wider public 'as Huxley and Tyndall did occasionally for science', 'to relax (where it can with decency be done) the austere repression of their emotions; that their writings may at least cheer "if they do not inebriate"'.

Chapter VI

Life at the School

All too little information has come to hand about the less formal aspects of the School in its early decades. The Athens archive includes cabinet photographs of men in cap and gown (Gardner), tall stiff collars (Tod, Loring), or carefully posed with the tools of their trade on the Finlay balcony (a rich series, including Margaret Hardie, Hasluck, Thompson, Tillyard, Wace and Toynbee); and romantic portraits of Eugenie Sellars (Mrs Strong), Gisela Richter and Hilda Lorimer which give a rather misleading impression of the mental and physical calibre of these distinguished scholars. One splendid group photograph of a Christmas play, in remarkably varied and exotic costumes, which includes the Director (Harcourt Smith) and his wife, tells us a little about one of their diversions. Before the Hostel was built some students had to live in the town; it is likely that some were accommodated in the Upper House, at least at first, and ailing students were well cherished by the wives of Directors there. At first the Hostel staff included a butler, but how long this grand-sounding arrangement lasted is unrecorded.

Mrs Bosanquet, though a Somervillian and familiar from girlhood with academics, found the students rather stiff and silent, especially by comparison with their socially more out-going contemporaries at the American School. On their own ground, however, they were less serious; Wace's all too few reminiscences (handed on by his daughter Elizabeth French) included spoof lectures held on winter evenings. All had to take part, and among the visitors the Germans were particularly talented. Karo came disguised as a Fräulein, while others were dressed as statues. The text of one lecture has been miraculously preserved among Kurt Müller's papers; it is reproduced as Appendix III for connoisseurs of archaeological take-offs. The tennis court, constructed in 1906 on American initiative, provided another field for friendly rivalry. The students were often invited to dinner and other functions at the Legation, where the Bosanquets, firm friends, dined about twice a week; the Royal Ladies, too, saw a good deal of Mrs Bosanquet, and Marcus Tod acted as tutor to one of the Princes.

This is perhaps the place to write of the School's women students who, though admitted from very early days (Eugenie Sellars in 1890, Amy Hutton in 1896), were not permitted to reside, or to work on excavations. However they were funded, it was not by official studentships. This was contemplated in 1903, but did

Margaret Hardie (later Hasluck), School Student 1911

not actually arise until 1910, when M. M. Hardie of Newnham College was nominated for the School Studentship by the Cambridge Vice-Chancellor. As the School was contemplating an excavation in Turkey (at Datcha) at the time, 'the question was raised [in the Managing Committee] whether ladies prudently could take part in excavations in the Ottoman Empire'. Margaret Hardie got her studentship and, though the Datcha dig did not come off, went on to work with Sir William Ramsay in Anatolia. But the question of School Studentships for women came up again in 1912 in a more acute form when the Committee was re-drafting the letters in which these were offered to the Vice-Chancellors of Oxford and Cambridge; the wording was, correctly, criticised by Jane Harrison (the Hellenic Society representative on the Committee) as excluding women, since it referred to those eligible as 'members of the University'. After considerable debate — and Miss Harrison was prepared to bring the matter before a General Meeting of Subscribers if the Committee could not agree — the wording was adjusted to give expression to the Committee's opinion that 'while the Studentship was originally founded for members of the University, there is nothing on the side of the School to bar the admission of women, if the University in the exercise of its discretion thinks fit to interpret the offer in the wide sense'. As a footnote it may be observed that Amy Hutton, who had already done sterling service as Assistant Editor of the *Annual*, was acting as Secretary to the Committee in the session 1911–12! As for excavations, Winifred Lamb, in this as in much else a pioneer, was later to prove that in post-Ottoman Turkey women could not only take part in but organise excavations on Turkish soil.

A possible first step in the admission of women to the Hostel (Directors had always had their wives with them in the Upper House) was prevented by the outbreak of war in 1914. The Assistant Director Hasluck, then lately married (to Margaret Hardie), asked permission for his wife to live in with him. Jane Harrison urged a favourable reply, as a trial 'whether the presence of ladies resident in the Hostel would not work well'. But the general feeling of the Committee was hostile; 'in the long run the men would certainly feel less comfortable than they had hitherto', and with the outbreak of war the Assistant Directorship lapsed.

Because the women students lived outside the School it must not be assumed that they were only seen there in the Library or the 'ladies' sitting-room', or in the Director's house (as a baby Charles Bosanquet was pushed in his pram by Gisela Richter). Before the Hasluck marriage, the very reasonable tendency of archaeologists to marry each other was exemplified by Guy Dickins and Mary Hamilton. This tendency accelerated, no doubt, after women students came to live in the Hostel — Ruby Woodley later estimated the incidence of School marriages as an average of one a year — but was not so common that that crusted old bachelor Duncan Mackenzie could not refer to the news of the Pendleburys' engagement as 'that scandal at the School in Athens'.

In the first full session after the war a combination of factors opened the Hostel to women. The bachelor students were few, and married students, the Ashmoles for instance, like single women had to live out. The considerable political upheaval in Athens over the return of King Constantine provided an excellent reason for the Director, with strong support from the Legation, to gather all his students into the Hostel, a move so successful that it was never again questioned. Proposals for a combined American/British women's hostel were made from the American side at intervals over the next seven years, but were never seriously considered by the Committee. By the time Loring Hall, with its separate megara for men and women, was completed in 1928, British women students formed a good proportion of Hostel residents; a married Assistant Director, Heurtley, lived as of right in the Hostel, as did his successors until the provision of a separate Assistant Director's flat. Only in 1935–6 did an excess of students in the British School cause two of the women — and one man — to find lodging and a cordial welcome in Loring Hall.

Such glimpses as can be caught of life in the Hostel before 1914 present the familiar picture of good fellowship — Arnold Toynbee speaks appreciatively of the helpful kindness shown to him by those of longer standing — learned joking and name-calling (H. J. W. Tillyard was universally known as the Physiodoule), and tough travel. Maurice Thompson assured the writer that he and Wace would simply put a toothbrush in the pocket of their waterproofs and so set off to Thessaly.

From December 1920 there is Lilian Chandler's diary to give a fresh and vivid picture of British School life. Greece was bitterly divided, her resources of every kind heavily committed to the war against Turkey in Asia Minor. Roads were in chronic disrepair, trains ran late or not at all owing to frequent breakdowns. The only effect of these material disadvantages on the constant journeyings of the students was to increase their resourcefulness and adaptability. Were they benighted in the more distant parts of Attica? They would find lodging and hospitality (given, as always generously) with papades, monks or villagers. These contacts turned to friendships; the Papas of Vrana would visit the girls at the School; they would cherish the son of the Kako Salesi Grigos family in hospital in Athens. Most excursions were made largely on foot, and apparently at the normal School breakneck pace; 'we unfortunately did the 3 hours walk in $1\frac{1}{2}$ hours' going to Phyle, — though on an extended tour through Arcadia in a very wet spring the girls hired a guide with mules. Most of the longer excursions recorded were made by the two or three girls, but there was a mass exodus of seven students to Aegina, and for many of the Attic explorations they had the benefit of F. B. Welch's guidance. 'Mr Welch was the best company in the world, and knew more about mediaeval and modern Attica than even the Director himself. It was Mr Welch who introduced the students to places that were then little known and hard of access; he also told with relish the legends connected with some of them' (Winifred Lamb). Himself an old student (1898) and at the time Vice-Consul, he was living in the School to work on the Finlay papers.

At home in the Hostel, Mary Herford assumed the responsibilities of 'housekeeper-in-chief', holding her own against the formidable Kalliope. Christmas 1920 was preceded by communal pudding-making; 'we danced round it

Confrontation with the housekeeper 1920,
drawn by Winifred Lamb:
Welch, Mrs Ashmole, Bernard Ashmole,
Mary Herford, Miriam Chandler

and performed mystic rites to impress Kalliope; even Mr Wace joined in', and celebrated by dinner in the Director's house and a dance at the American School (the School's pudding was eaten on New Year's Eve, with Wace and Blegen as guests). The Granvilles at the Legation gave a dance, which the students much enjoyed, and were themselves guests at another given in the Upper House. Other social functions ranged from tea with Madame Schliemann to charades at the American School. An unusual but necessary exercise was 'caterpillar parade' early in January, to remove the procession caterpillar nests from the pine trees. Welch held the ladder, Wace climbed it, and the students disposed of the debris.

When not travelling, the students attended lectures in the National Museum with Wace, Acropolis Museum with Casson, and on the Acropolis with B. H. Hill. Renaudin lectured, on Thera pottery, at the French School, and Tsountas at the University. It is clear how much the students' life was enhanced by the presence of resident older scholars like Ashmole, Casson and Welch, and visitors like Austen Harrison and Leonard Woolley.

Heurtley's long period as Assistant Director provided an element of continuity and experience throughout the twenties. He was a good raconteur, with a fund of

Winifred Lamb
(photo, James Brock)

wartime stories, and a cross-country walker of the usual School kind. Most students of the later twenties spent some time on his digs in Macedonia; fewer took part in the School dig at Sparta. Winifred Lamb wrote of the happy atmosphere at these excavations; at Sparta this was partly due to the presence of Piet de Jong, who 'has more joy of life than almost anyone I know, and it was he who, unconsciously perhaps, made the party so merry and prevented undue despondency, when things were not going well, by his historic series of caricatures'. The Director (Woodward), too, described by another student as a 'shy, remote, kindly figure', enlivened proceedings by quiet humour. 'His Epigrams', Winifred remarks, 'are unfailingly good', and quotes a limerick, inspired by one of the warriors from the Aegina Aphaia temple pediment, which must strike a chord in the heart of anyone who travelled in pre-war Greece.

> There once was a Warrior, who said
> I think I've a bug in my bed;
> I'll take off my helmet
> And then overwhelm it,
> I can't get to sleep till it's dead.

As always, most students spent long stretches of time travelling, in conditions as difficult as those already recorded. Though the train service was now fairly reliable and punctual, roads were awful 'apart from on foot, the only way of travelling by road was to take a seat in a taxi, when one was jammed so tight against one's neighbours that one 'could not shake about'. Living in the country was cheap, but

Sylvia Benton in Ithaca, 1933

hotels moderate to awful. The School was still on the outskirts of Athens, and Lycabettus was in the country. Beyond it there was a vast shanty town of refugees from Asia Minor; between Athens and Phaleron was all open fields. Water was short but the School got enough; the completion in 1931 of the Marathon dam improved the supply but so increased the price that baths had to be strictly rationed.

'Spartan living and hard walking was the standard set by the Heurtleys' (Nicholas Hammond). From 1927 onwards a new generation of School cross-country 'runners' begins to appear, Bertrand Hallward, Sylvia Benton, John Pendlebury, Nicholas Hammond himself. Hallward first, who, reaching Greece overland, was impressed by his first glimpse of Parnassos, left the train, and climbed to the top of it. Charles Seltman, who travelled with him — but not up Parnassos — recalled the comment of awed Greek villagers at his energy, height and blonde beauty 'it is Apollo'. We catch an early glimpse of Sylvia's mettle on an expedition to Phyle; to Pendlebury's comment on the awful pace she set, she replied 'I like that, I had to run to keep up with you', but was in the van for most of the way. Earlier she had climbed Taygetos alone, and incurred the Director's wrath thereby. Pendlebury, an Olympic high jumper, showed his quality in mainland walking before going off to cover Crete, at breakneck speed, from end to end. At the end of a day's walk from Athens to Thebes he sprinted the last mile or so to delay the Orient Express for his companions (Hammond, Heurtley, Theodore Skeat). Poor Skeat, nicknamed The Horse, was rather out of his class on this occasion, but he was sufficiently tough to go with Heurtley and Hammond, in mid-winter and bitter cold, to walk up the Haliakmon gorge to Servia and later to Armenochori. On another excursion to Doris with Hammond, he is remembered as dressed in a suit and tie, ordinary shoes and carrying a suitcase. Hammond's own surveys in Epirus, both Greek and Albanian, stood him in good stead during the war years he spent with the British Mission to EAM/ELAS. One more record of this time; Hammond wished to demonstrate, in person, that the Athenian army could indeed have marched after the battle, on the same day, from Marathon to Athens. This he did by a round walk of 48 miles, six hours going, seven returning, over the summit of Pendeli to the *soros* and back.

The 'Spartan living' entailed of course hard work in libraries and museums; the students of those days were a self-contained community ('almost a family') and did not see members of the American School, go much down into Athens, or at all into Greek society. Mrs Heurtley did the Hostel catering, and on Heurtley's digs the cooking as well. Dilys Powell gives a vivid picture of the domestic problems of the Director's household (*The Traveller's Journey is done*, p. 45). Bedroom floors were bare, bedside lights non-existent; even after Gerard Young's refurbishing of the Hostel the Committee set its face against these, presumably regarding reading in bed with the same disapproval as Henry James' Mr Carteret. Mattresses were kapok; re-spun annually by a visiting craftsman, they left his hands soft and plump, but separated out into lumps over the rest of the year. There was a fire — tending to smoke — in the Finlay library, but no central heating except in the main library where until 1937 heat came from a cast-iron stove (as in an English parish church). Not surprisingly, some students took to exercise to keep warm; hockey was played in a mixed team, organised by Heurtley, of English residents, Greeks and some Cypriots, on the Panathenaic Football Ground — a very fast clay surface. Their opponents were usually Greek teams, and the Mediterranean Fleet sometimes fielded a side when on a visit. Other people took to roller skating, and there was always the tennis court.

During the middle to late thirties the School underwent a gradual but positive spiritual change — a softening, not of fibre or enterprise, but of the competitive toughness already noted. Three factors are perhaps identifiable among the reasons for this shift: the increased number of women students during these years, the generous refurbishing of the Hostel by Gerard Young, which made it for the first time for years — *expertae crede* — a comfortable place to live in, and the stability imparted to the pound-drachma exchange rate under the Metaxas regime. It may be, too, that the tragic deaths of Payne and Blakeway in 1936 suggested to those who made a principle of living and travelling as uncomfortably as possible the wisdom of sometimes taking a little care.

Arriving, in 1935, after a four or five-days journey, a student was first introduced to the two ancient and temperamental geysers, sole sources of hot water and not infrequently of explosions. Next the neophyte was despatched (via Kolonaki where remarkably dim copies of passport photographs had to be acquired) to apply, in such faltering Greek as he or she possessed, for passes for museums and railways, and to secure, from the chaos of the Aliens Bureau, a residence permit. At meals, he or she must learn to take portions exactly adjusted to the numbers present; meals were served formally, though occasionally very slow eaters, of tangerines for example, were allowed a head start.

Pleasures were at first communal; as a body, the School went to swim off the then empty headlands of Glyphada or Vouliagmeni; *en masse* it climbed (some with marked reluctance, others at a run) the prickly slopes of Hymettus. It was Robert Beaumont who carried a cup of water from Kaisariani to the summit, to drink with lunch, John Cook and Enid Robertson who scorned a shorter way home than via St. John the Hunter. These three were concerned in a high proportion of the tougher excursions; Enid could even emerge from an all-night journey on deck with sheep looking clean and ready for anything. With Eric Gray, Robert and Tom Dunbabin she took part in the mid-winter climb of Dirphis, which started at Chalkis and ended in the small hours at Kyme, where they nearly missed the boat to Piraeus. It was early in May that Tom and Robert set out for the top of Ida with one House scarf and a cucumber between them (they accepted a rug from Doreen (not then Dunbabin) before actually starting).

By Christmas the School had separated into groups; it was overpopulated, with members of the British School at Rome — which was temporarily in voluntary exile owing to sanctions against the Italian war in Abyssinia — also to be accommodated, and bed occupation constantly rotating; Betty Dunkley (Wedeking) recalls that the first time she saw Ellis Waterhouse (the Rome School Librarian) he was asleep in what she had hoped was still her bed! Daytime visitors often included Berthe Segal, Peter Kahane (later expelled from the Austrian Institute after the Anschluss and admitted officially to student privilege) and Willy Schwabacher, whom Nazi policy made unwelcome at the German or Austrian Institutes. To make space, Betty and the writer were transferred to Loring Hall (where the Womens Megaron was almost empty); doubly fortunate, they acquired transatlantic ties and avoided the spasmodic Oxford-Cambridge bickering which marred the later months of the Session. There was no School dig to take people out of Athens, though everyone travelled a great deal from February onwards. For sea travel deck was *de rigueur*, and indeed in warm weather much preferable. Whichever boat one happened to be on, the evening procession out of Piraeus, the race down the Saronic Gulf to the accompaniment of competitive hooting, and the final branching of the sea routes never failed of their excitement.

The session 1936-7 shines in memory as one of those periods, rare in anyone's life, when a whole group was united in general good-fellowship — not that rivalry, mockery, special attachments were lacking, but on the whole everyone enjoyed everyone else's company. Even the incessant ping-pong (that season's way of keeping warm) was quite often of the communal, progressive, variety. The champion was Vincent Desborough, whose match, in later days, against the Greek table-tennis champion of Germany (where he had been a student) was epic; the enemy arrived with his own two bats, but Vincent so skilfully exploited the bevelled edges of the School table — none of your proper tables there! — that the match ended in the stupefied defeat of the visitor. The overall friendliness had its drawbacks for the patient restaurants of Athens, for on Sunday evenings the School would dine, and play, in large groups not innocent of spillikins competitions with tooth-picks (it was an unexpected pleasure to read that in her day Winifred Lamb had behaved similarly) or noisier diversions. A happy memory is of looking on while Vincent and John Griffith (later Oxford's Public Orator) ate a meal backwards, from coffee to soup, in the prim surroundings of Costi's.

Studentships — perhaps this is the point to observe that their value was from £100 to £200 — went further with a stable drachma, and more people were able to travel outside Greece proper, to Cyprus, Egypt, the Dodecanese, Istanbul and Troy; much of the Turkish coast was a military zone, and inaccessible; Arthur Beattie went, in 1938, to study Galatian inscriptions, but never managed to see more than the outsides of locked boxes containing them. Work in Italian museums was made financially easier by the large reductions on the Italian railways obtainable by a short visit to the Fascist *Mostra* in Rome (it was possible to get from Athens to Oxford in this way for under £12).

As in earlier sessions, life was enriched by extended visits from older scholars, and in May 1937 the Director entertained the Chairman himself, accompanied by Professor Fränkel. Ears straining not to miss a word of the rapid flow of anecdote, the students accompanied them, Myres riding patriarchally on a donkey, to sites and museums. The School's Patron, H.R.H. the Duke of Kent, in Athens for his marriage to Princess Marina, took tea with the Director and the students; Austin St. Barbe Harrison, Arnold Gomme and Bernard Ashmole were other visitors. Musical functions took place in the Upper House, especially when Gerard Young, himself an excellent and powerful trained baritone, had Astra Desmond as his guest. Their duets more than filled the *saloni*, and walls and windows took considerable strain.

Perhaps under the shadow of Munich, or by the accidents of friendships, from 1938 more ties developed with the Legation and the British community; the Anglo-Hellenic League and young British Council, both close at hand, were other factors. Wallace Southam (of Shell) organised part-singing meetings which were good enough to produce a Christmas concert of carols at the Anglo-Hellenic League. Several students took part, including Vincent and Vronwy Fisher. They also played with the Shell hockey team, of which the table-tennis champion was centre forward; 'he believed in the power of intimidation to defeat opponents, and used to rush their defence, yelling' (Vronwy Hankey). The Italian invasion of Albania, in April 1939, inspired contingency plans for students to be employed on war work at the Legation. It also brought to Athens Mrs Hasluck, whose Intelligence record in the first war made her continued residence at Elbasan rather hazardous. Her fame preceded her; on an earlier visit (1934) when she stayed some weeks in the Hostel, she had alarmed the shyer spirits by exclaiming 'there isn't one of you dear boys I couldn't marry' (Robert Cook says she made one exception). But on this occasion she stayed in Kephissia for the summer, in only intermittent contact with the School. (Heard at dinner; 'what I like about you, Mr Dunbabin, is that you always speak to me as to my husband's widow'.)

The outbreak of war, seen as inevitable from the moment the Hitler-Stalin pact was signed, found the School very full, mostly with summer visitors. Dunbabin was in Athens, and Wace and his party of excavators hurried back from Mycenae, except for one of the architects, Wulf Schäfer (a quarter-Jew), who, after agonised days of indecision, had returned to his ungrateful fatherland; Mrs Hasluck moved down from Kephissia. Once it seemed clear that Italy intended to remain non-belligerent for the immediate future, visitors and those members of the School who had jobs in England, or early hopes of entering the armed forces, left for home. They were followed later in September by Dunbabin, when it became clear, after the Director's return to Athens, that his hopes that the School might continue to function as a learned institution were not to be realised.

As in the first war, the School became effectually an extension of the Legation. The Library was occupied by the Department of Information and the Press; Young (most private of men) presided over this as Director of Publicity, with David Wallace in charge of the Press section, and the Miss Woodleys running the office. The remaining students, absorbed into various sections of the Legation, were joined in residence by miscellaneous Legation personnel — the more prestigious, like the Caccias (First Secretary) were put up by the Director — and a large group of British Council staff, nearly all, by some curious quirk of appointment, impassioned phoneticians. Gerald Macpherson, a Canadian pupil of Homer Thompson, arrived too late to find the School in working order.

Spring 1940 brought the Binyons, he to lecture as Byron Professor, Robin Burn and Mary, to reorganise a somewhat tense British council, and John Pendlebury, disguised as a civilian but with a rich repertory of Cavalry stories from Weedon, and songs whose refrain tended to show that 'the horse is always right'. All too soon he moved on to Crete, whence he emitted those legendary telegrams ('am having cypher books rebound, binder believed reliable') which worked off some of his impatience with diplomatic protocol. Archaeology was upheld by Vronwy Fisher, who assisted Hutchinson to dig a chamber tomb near the Temple Tomb before leaving for home, and Wace, who spent all his time out of the Passport Control Office helping in another excavation, the great work of packing up the National Museum collections for safe storage.

The phoneticians, except for Julian Pring (later author of the excellent Modern Greek dictionaries) who stayed until the evacuation of April 1941, moved out of the Hostel, but phonetics did not. A frequent visitor to Mrs. Hasluck was a young

Albanian, Frederick, with whom she conversed on folklore and philology; the latter, and the Albanian language, seemed to an idle ear to consist largely of the syllable pop; 'pop-pop; pop-pop-pop'.

Italy's entry into the war brought an increased work-load and reduced the numbers of the archaeological community. Most of the Americans sailed away, taking with them Helen Wace and Lisa, leaving in Athens only the Gorham Stevens, the Webers at the Gennadion, the Parsons and Rodney Young, and at Marousi the Vanderpools who, during the hungry winter to come, organised a life-preserving *syssition* for Greek children. The diminished band in the Hostel were joined by two naval officers (in mufti of course), whose access to NAAFI provided a welcome enlargement of its meagre commons; the elder, who was short and remarkably unassuming, emerged in the hectic days of April 1941 in the four-gold-ringed uniform of a Royal Navy Captain, with authority and calm to match.

The impact of Greece's entry into the war in October was immediate discomfort — the blackout, the alerts, the instant shortages of everything that accompany the total mobilisation of a poor country — followed by growing exhilaration as the flags flew and the bells rang for Greek victories. (Olivia Manning, who spent a few weeks in the School after escaping from Bucharest, gives a misleading impression of the 'feel' of this whole period in her Balkan Trilogy.) Full moons brought bomber crews from Egypt, British naval vessels sailed up the Saronic Gulf, old friends returned in uniform. As winter yielded to spring, the observant walker, bound for Hymettus, would sight clusters of New Zealand or Australian soldiers encamped under the pines. The sweet-natured housemaid Georgia, desperate at hearing no word for three months from her soldier husband, set off one afternoon with a bagful of stones 'to throw at the Italians' — prisoners swarming in the barracks towards Ambelokepi. 'Well Georgia, did you hit any?' 'I couldn't bring myself to throw, they looked so miserable'.

From the short German campaign in mainland Greece two events have remained memorable; the enormous bang which shook everyone from bed when the Clan Fraser, loaded with ammunition, blew up in Piraeus on the first night; and an utterly cheering visit from Stanley Casson. The British Mission had by then retreated to Thebes so he came to call, bringing a captured Stahlhelm which fitted the Finlay Library bust of Homer to a T and remained on his head until the School was evacuated on 22nd April. A short pause in Western Crete contributed a vignette of the Director, exhilarated by the beauty of the countryside and good Cretan wine, striding across the hills (and startling the Cretan families who had already sought refuge in the surrounding caves) and debating whether he should not proceed to the Villa Ariadne and enquire why the King of Greece (pausing there on his own evacuation) had not asked his permission to stay in it.

From 1942 to 1944 the School housed the Swiss-Swedish Red Cross Mission, under Judge Sandström, whose food distributions saved so many Greek lives; their offices were in the Upper House. The return of the Greek Government to Athens in October 1944 was of course accompanied by the British Ambassador and his staff, several of whom, including the Burns, resided in the Hostel. There they sat out the hostilities of that sad December and January, at first without heat (they thinned out some of the garden pines), electricity, or water, for which they drew on a well in the American School garden. Rations were brought by army lorry from Piraeus every nine days or so, and were supplemented by dandelions from the garden and vitamin pills. Liberal dosing with mepacrine, against malaria, turned them all as yellow as jaundice sufferers. Things eased after the cease-fire on January 16th, and the Burns contributed to the task of reconciliation by parties, given in the Upper House, where Greek friends, estranged from one another by war and politics, could meet on neutral ground.

British army units were still in Greece until 1946. From November 1945 courses on the archaeology and history of Greece were organised by the army education authorities, and held in the Payne Room. As a consequence some ninety service personnel applied for and received permission to read in the Library. It was in the spring of 1946 that the first Greek General Elections for ten years were held, their fairness to be guaranteed by the presence of American, French and British Observers. Preliminary courses in Greek history and similar subjects were held in parallel in Naples, in February, for the observers, who may well have included some of the ninety.

The School re-opened in the autumn of 1946. The buildings were in a bad state of repair — there had been a fire in the heating system of the Upper House — and the Hostel except for the Library and office was still occupied by Embassy staff, who also had some basement rooms in the Director's house until the end of March 1947. At Knossos, the Villa Ariadne was occupied by the British Commanding Officer and his family under the vigilant eye of Manoli; the Hutchinsons with Kosti and Maria were at the Taverna but went home for the winter months. In Athens the session opened with only the Cooks in residence; Miss Woodley finally retired to England at the beginning of November and had no immediate successor. Eleni Kandaraki began her long association with the School as cook (and right-hand woman) in the Upper House. The Librarian arrived late in November to find the tables covered in parcels containing the Evans Bequest. To catalogue these and find places for them on the chronically overcrowded shelves was the first urgent task, the second to prepare for the binders some 150 books and periodicals. Despite the sepulchral chill of the library, unheated through one of the coldest, windiest and wettest Attic winters in memory, outside scholars came to read in it. (So did a mad mother cat, resident in the Hostel, whose ambition was to file her kittens there or in the sherd collection, but could seldom remember, when arriving with the second, where she had left the first.)

Archaeological company was not lacking. Semni and Christos Karouzos were living nearby and both French and American Schools were active; in 1947 excavations were proceeding both in the Agora and at Corinth. In May — to anticipate a little — the School acted for three weeks as headquarters for a party of students from the Swedish Institute in Rome and Eric Sjöqvist was its guest. The day Einar Gjerstad was entertained to lunch remains memorable for an explosion in the oil cooker which blew Eleni (unharmed) across the kitchen.

At the end of January Hutchinson and Hilda Pendlebury paused at the School on their way to Crete; there Hilda was at last able to establish those facts about John's death which had been so long in doubt (see the *Mémoire* and Dilys Powell, *The Villa Ariadne* p. 121ff. In mid-February, over night, the rain stopped, the sun shone, and it was spring. The new School Secretary, Sylvia Apostolidou, took up her (part-time) appointment, and travel, to the Argolid, to Crete, to Delphi (but not to areas still afflicted with civil war) became possible, but only with a police permit.

Students old and new arrived; Sylvia Benton and Anne Jeffery first, then Geoffrey Kirk and, later, Jock Anderson, still up at Oxford. Tom Dunbabin came in June to represent the Hellenic Society at the French School centenary celebrations, John Griffith came in July and had to sleep in the garden. Vincent Desborough, wearing still his British Council hat, was at hand all the winter and in June began to spend more time at the School preparing to take over the Librarianship — which, in the session 1947–8 he combined with being Assistant Director. In repeated visits to Ithaca (train to Patras, eight hours on by caique) Sylvia Benton finished the re-ordering of the Stavros Museum and made great progress with the far larger problem of the finds from Aetos, inadequately housed in Vathy.

The hostel was handed back to the School on the 3rd August and repairs and redecoration started at once. After a series of terrific *glendes* the Squire relinquished the Curatorship of Knossos and left Crete (with many very awkward packages of farewell presents!) in September.

At this point, a glance may be spared for the external circumstances in which the School was to begin again to function fully. Much of mainland Greece was still racked by Civil war and its aftermath, and travel permits were required for almost any journey. The Corinth Canal was still impassable, filled with destroyed rolling-stock by the departing Germans; not all the mines had been swept from the Aegean, so island communication, by caiques or ex-naval vessels, was only by daylight. In Athens water was restricted to certain hours, food was scarce and expensive, the School relying largely on NAAFI for supplies. This was one aspect of a new and closer relationship with the Embassy which helped to alleviate the difficulties of everyday living by cashing cheques, bag facilities and general support; the School was included in official visits, for example that of L. S. Amery in 1947, personal friendships were established with diplomatic staff and their families. Air travel was restricted, and the only access route for students was by sea from Marseilles, on which the Lykiardopoulos line gave them concessionary fares. The railway to the north was still out of commission, so that to get to Salonica one went by boat.

'Our students really are a lively crowd' wrote John Cook early in this first full session, and this enthusiasm is reflected in their reminiscences. All write with appreciation of the thoughtful kindness and helpfulness of the School officials and domestic staff, Desborough's care and tactful management being particularly remembered. From the summer of 1948 the Smyrna dig took the Director and a fair proportion of students away from Athens each year. The wives of Assistant Directors and senior students, though 'not to create a precedent', lived in the Hostel and are remembered as 'organising such pleasant social rituals as celebrating birthdays by importing enormously rich cakes for tea in the Finlay', and making curtains for bedrooms and covers for the Finlay chairs. They also embellished the garden and helped in the library — Sheila Boardman was particularly thanked for her work in mounting and labelling the photographic collection — and still made time to teach English in Athens to make ends meet. Though the exacting task of Assistant Director was no doubt alleviated, especially for those with young children, by the provision of a flat above the Annexe (1957), it is difficult not to feel that something was thereby lost to the life of the Hostel; the other side of the coin was the facility it gave for keeping open house, as the Huxleys are remembered doing, for Greek acquaintance and friends, and other colleagues. Authoritative pronouncements — 'Gentlemen do not discuss pot-handles at breakfast' (Philip Sherrard) — were no longer available at every meal to curb dedicated prehistorians.

The appointment of Visiting Fellow, long desired, was first made in 1953 (Nicholas Hammond), but in almost any session the number of 'old' students tended to be equal to or greater than that of newcomers, and their help and counsel was a valued part of life at the School. From 1950, for 25 years, Jane Rabnett, secretary, accountant, assistant librarian, was everybody's friend and resource; at her appointment the Director is said to have commented that her previous experience on the staff of a Borstal establishment would stand her in good stead at the School!

From 1948 there were students again at the American School (mainly girls), and they were to be found both at the parties in the Finlay, which often also included staff of the British Council, and at the evenings in tavernas, for which, western dancing not being allowed in public, the students prepared by learning Greek dances. John Boardman writes: 'The American School played a very important part in the academic life of students as well as the social. They were invited to join groups being taken round Athens (days with Rodney Young in the Agora, etc.). With all Greek museums still closed the only way to see and handle objects was in the Agora, where we were generously given free run of the shelves and were able to learn much from the regular American staff there, Homer Thompson, Gene Vanderpool, Missie Crosbie, Virginia Grace, and not least Lucy Talcott.' Semni Karouzou too, involved in the heavy task of re-establishing the collections of the National Museum showed much kindness to members of the School.

In the middle fifties the quality of life in the Hostel suffered from the pressure of numbers (183 admissions to Student Privilege in 1952/3), and even the restriction on admissions for a year during the early part of the prolonged troubles over Cyprus made only a short dint. Hotheads, in January 1956, were threatening to burn down the School, and a policeman was stationed 'for protection' at the lower gate, but travellers in country places — and at this period much time was spent in travel — rarely met with anything but friendliness. In Athens there was some official coldness. There was as yet not much contact with the reconstituted German and Italian Institutes, but students were in constant friendly relations with the American School, where one Assistant Director (C. W. J. Eliot) returned with an English wife whom he had found at the School. David Lewis comments: 'It would be legitimate for the historian, if so inclined, to note the importance of the tennis court in the development of affairs (or what then passed for them) between the British and American Schools'; John Graham wrote of 'the American girls next door whose presence added to the gaiety of the place and the quality of our tennis'. Connections with the Embassy and British Council were thriving, and there was a picnic one Boxing Day on top of Pendeli to which the Ambassador invited the School. Both the Directors of the period were generous hosts, and at least one Easter lamb roast in the Upper House garden went on from 11 a.m. until 6 p.m.

It was however a period of great financial stringency all round (as noted above) and the discomfort this entailed for Hostel residents was acute in the winter. Brian Sparkes writes: 'The lack of heat is what I chiefly remember (1956–7). . . particularly within the library where we sat in our sleeping bags; baths were a headache; if one member had a bath too early in the evening that was all the water gone, whereas a little later in the evening it might be possible for three to have the luxury of a hot bath. Cockroaches came up the pipes in the washbasins. . . There was always yoghourt for breakfast, and iced water for the warmer weather had to be fetched from the fridge in the kitchen'. Overall, however, students of this time look back to their stay in Athens 'as a marvellously rich and rewarding period', and to the School as an ideal place to work for anyone interested in ancient Greece, a source of valuable friendships and interesting acquaintances.

In the early sixties numbers declined; the Visiting Fellow, in the spring of 1961, noted only one full-time student not of senior status using the library — though others were probably working in Crete at the time. No doubt finance was largely responsible, and indeed another Visiting Fellow remarks that 'the poverty-stricken state of the School is universally commented upon in Athens'. It became a matter of policy that students' wives should be encouraged to live in the Hostel, and if possible be employed on School work, to relieve their husbands of undue financial strain. Yet by 1964 the Hostel was full, students were living out, and there was heavy pressure on all facilities, on reading space in the library, and dining space at meals. Mrs. Zafeiri, installed as Housekeeper in 1961, and her staff were fully extended and, on the administrative level, both Philip Sherrard, the Assistant Director, and Jane Rabnett were stretched to the limit. New categories of student were introduced, priority of accommodation being given to full students, and occupants of the rooms in the Annexe having no right to use the dining-room or Finlay library. Associate students in any case often came to Greece only to assist at specific excavations, which full students were no longer under obligation to do, as the School Student at least had once been.

With better funding from 1962, the Hostel grew more comfortable; easy chairs, table lamps, interior-spring mattresses became standard, the central heating system was extended to the bedrooms. Comparable improvements and conveniences like washing machines were installed in the domestic quarters. Looking back, in 1968, over five years that had seen extensions to both Library and Hostel, Hugh Sackett comments on the improved amenities, the more professional air in the running of the Hostel, the greater comfort for the residents. At Knossos too the Taverna was under constant enlargement and improvement as the pressure of rescue work there continued to demand the presence of more archaeologists to supervise it. For those who remember the Villa Ariadne before the war it is strange and, in a way sad, to read that, when it was made available for British diggers in 1968, its accommodation was described as 'very poor; students would have been better off in any average workman's house in the village'; but happy too to think what this meant for the prosperity of the Knossian workmen.

It is not clear why, during the sixties, students came to feel oppressed by formality in the Hostel, especially at meals. In earlier days the Assistant Director, or Senior Student, sat at the head of the table, but the rest sat as chance dictated; there was no special occasion for inviting visitors, who were normally properly introduced — for an exception, one may record Waterhouse's greeting to Sylvia Benton, arriving late: 'you must be the notorious Miss Benton'. Dressing for dinner was, in spite of Miss Woodley's efforts, more honoured in the breach than in the observance. Yet the 1968 Visiting Fellow records 'after consultation. . . it was agreed that formality as to dress, processing in and out and seating positions should be relaxed for lunch. Dinner to be as before, with Thursday night's meals suitable for guests, with better food'. This modification had taken place by 1971, when Frank Stubbings observed that 'a family atmosphere still prevails', and noted specifically the agreeable atmosphere at meals and the cheerful dining-room murals painted by two resident artists. Formal meals are nowadays a thing of the past, and a good deal of self-help is expected of residents, especially at weekends.

David Lewis noted, about 1956, 'a good deal of joking about the uselessness of everyone else's subjects', and 'a predominance of persons devoted to pottery' — though not yet the overwhelming numbers of prehistorians. An innovation of Peter Warren's years as Assistant Director was the institution of informal seminars held during the winter months to keep students *au fait* with one another's subjects. These proved so useful a bridge between the ever-widening range of subjects studied, and the simultaneous need to specialise to fulfil the requirements of the thesis system, that they became a regular feature of the winter months. This same system, involving frequent contact with a supervisor in England, may have been responsible for the very uneven number of residents in the earlier months of each session. The apparent under-use of the, now very extensive, facilities caused considerable anxiety to the Committee, especially in the years round 1970, and successful efforts were made to attract to Athens students of a wider range of disciplines. As their fields of study spread, so did the provenance of the students.

Australians were very well represented, even after the foundation of their own School in 1980; distinguished representatives have been Jill Carington Smith, Knossos Fellow for several years, and Roger Just, Assistant Director 1980–1984. Canadians are represented, though they earlier tended to become members of the American School; they now have their own School but as yet no accommodation for students. Students have come from Japan, India, Sri Lanka, Ghana and South Africa; Swedes, Swiss, Dutch, Danish and Belgians have been wecome for many years, but since 1977 the Swiss and the Dutch, like the Swedes, have had their own institutions in Athens. In recent years the School has been happy to include scholars from Yugoslavia.

A major change in the life of the Hostel after 1975 was the retirement of Jane Rabnett — not too far, she has a house in Naxos. Some formal acknowledgement of the value of her work and presence in the School was shown by the conferment of the MBE in 1973, but the regard and affection of generations of its members cannot be measured.

Not surprisingly, the problem for the late seventies and the 1980s became, again, that of numbers; the presence (in 1980–81) of twenty students simultaneously in residence, made possible only by using the Annexe all the year round and for full students, proved unacceptable. The problem extended also to Knossos where, in 1982, there were at times more people in residence than in Athens. With such numbers, the dining-room was cramped and meals at times inadequate, supplemented for the less dedicated by evenings of pizza and poker in the Finlay. In spite of the inevitable tensions, increased in the summer months by the ebb and flow of visitors needing advice and guidance, general good-fellowship prevailed, with people going on trips and out to dinner in large groups. The more valuable Finlay books having been removed for safety to the Office, including, alas, the beloved travel volumes, more room was made by taking away the bookshelves from the southern wall, and the room was done over, special, personalised, cushions being presented by the Athens secretary Helen Clark. Mrs Anna Zapheiri, having celebrated her 21st year as Housekeeper in 1982, retired the following year after a splendid leaving party. The moving tribute to her in the Annual Report for 1982–3 is too long to be reproduced here but one sentence may be quoted; 'She saw the School as her home, its members as part of her extended family; when you know that you begin to understand the real nature of Mrs Zapheiri's Housekeepership. It will not be forgotten'. At first her successor, Mrs. Phanara did not live in the Hostel (the domestic staff also have lived out for some years); since, however, she and her daughters have made it their home.

1981 was the year of the earthquake, which did the School little damage, of a great mix of nationalities and a surprising wealth of students of Byzantine topics. The closest external contacts on a personal level were with Swedish and Italian students; some School members went on the American School trips, others on day trips organised by the Macmillan Student about three times a session. Most students attended the tour of Roman monuments in Athens run by the Director, and tours of other Athenian monuments organised by the American School. One excitement was the discovery in a chest in the hall of 'world war II bombs', which must in fact have been bomb cases, from Spitfire attacks on ELAS in the Stadium during the *Dekembriana*, collected by Robin Burn and presented to the School in 1975. Guest nights were re-introduced in 1981–2, but the informal character and early hour of the evening meal militated against the frequent entertainment of Greek visitors. Festivities included a fancy-dress party for Carnival, a bonfire party for Guy Fawkes night, and the annual splendid all-day lamb roast in the Upper House garden.

Like all human institutions, the School at Athens has its ups and downs, combinations of circumstance and character which make its life more, or less, harmonious and rewarding. Alumni, visiting for short periods, may return saying sadly 'students nowadays do — or do not — this or that'; Visiting Fellows, who stay longer, tend to see the persistence in the present of characteristics and atmosphere which they remember with respect and affection. Many changes are real and permanent, the increased number of School officers, the 'daily' character of domestic service, the impact of huge changes in Athens and Greece itself. The essence of the School, however, and this does not change, is that its members, of proved intelligence, have chosen to come to it, because there best of all they can pursue some piece of work of intellectual interest to themselves and, it is hoped, some importance to the sum of knowledge.

Appendix I

Greek Government Decree

Translation from the Official Gazette of June 3, 1884.

Royal Decree concerning the grant of a building site belonging to the Monastery of Petraki for the erection of an English Archaeological School.

George I

King of the Hellenes

Upon the proposal of our Minister of Ecclesiastical Affairs and Public Instruction, we sanction the Act of the Council of the Monastery of Assomatos or Petraki, numbered 2618 and dated 11/23 May of this year, by which a building lot is granted to the English Archaeological School to be established at Athens, and to be represented by the Minister of Great Britain in the same city. The building lot is situated at Athens near the above mentioned monastery and at the western side of the same having the following boundaries. To the eastward the olive grove and grounds belonging to the monastery; to the westward the nameless street and ground belonging to the normal school, to the north ground belonging to the monastery, and to the south the hospital Evangelismos, a street, and the ground of the monastery. Its extent is of 6 Royal Stremma and 145 square metres as per plan submitted to us, and it will serve for the erection of the English Archaeological School.

The above named Minister is charged with the execution and publication of this Decree, and is moreover requested to express to the above-mentioned Council of the Monastery our due appreciation for this grant.

ATHENS, May 18/30, 1884.
(Signed) GEORGE.
(Signed) D. S. VOULPIOTI
Minister for Ecclesiastical Affairs,

etc., etc., etc.,

Appendix II
Advice to Students

METHODS OF WORK AND TEACHING

Extracted from a recent report of the present Director to the Managing Committee

Under an ideal system most students would spend two, some three, seasons in Greece, devoting *the first year to general studies, the second to some special subject.*

During the first year a man need not lose sight of his special subject, but in most cases it would pay him to adopt something like the following programme:

(August and) *September.* In Berlin (Munich, Dresden) to become familiar with spoken German and so be able to profit by some of the 3 or 4 courses of lectures given by the Secretaries of German and Austrian Institutes.

October. Arrive in Greece. Face the difficulties of language and travelling. See Olympia, Delphi, Mycenae, Epidaurus, the Heraeum near Argos, before the rains begin in November.

About *November* 15. Settle down in Hostel for 3 or 4 months of steady work on sites and in Museums, attending some of the half-dozen available courses of lectures, and making frequent short excursions into the country, by train, bicycle, carriage, or on mule-back. A bicycle is invaluable.

This residence in the Hostel, with occasional absences for a few nights in the country, should last until the beginning or middle of March according to the season.

March, April. Travel, study ancient sites.

If possible join one of the island-cruises to which Professor Gardner and Professor Dörpfeld have hospitably admitted students in the past.

May, June. Begin to concentrate attention on special work: e.g. a man may assist in excavation, with a view to working upon the results during the coming year and excavating with more or less complete control or independence in his second summer: or he may explore a given district in Greece or Asia Minor, and island or group of islands: or he may work his way homewards through a number of Museums in Italy, Austria and Germany: or attend Mau's summer course of lectures at Pompeii and afterwards spend some months in Rome and the cooler Etruscan cities. In the latter case he will do well to attach himself to the British School at Rome (Palazzo Odescalchi), where a library is being formed and advice and information may be obtained.

For the *second year* it is impossible to formulate a definite scheme. It should be devoted almost entirely to special work in a narrower field.

The course here suggested must be modified in different ways to suit each case. There will always be men who, like most of the French students, are already specialists in some branch of classical learning and only seek fresh material for research. On the other hand there will be others who wish to see something of all sides of ancient life, to visit sites and battle fields, illuminating and colouring their past reading and fitting themselves for general classical teaching, but have no time for minute archaeological studies.

It is evident that in each year the methods and matter of the teaching at the School must be adapted to the requirements of the students. Students from English universities will never have the love of formal lectures which distinguishes those from America, and where the numbers are small it will often be better to teach, as Dr. Wolters has been in the habit of doing, by means of informal visits to sites and museums.

Appendix III
Mock Lecture

(Found among the papers of Kurt Müller at Gottinger by Hurtmuth Dohl, with a list of slide numbers [presumably referring to the German Institute collection] and these drawings).

A project for an international dig at Herculaneum had apparently been mooted. The tablet, of course, is Minoan.

BSA 15/2/09

My ladies and my gentlemen

I am very glad to have the honour to speak to this illustrious congregation, and I thank you for the friendly ear you will kindly give me. On the other hand, the excavations we made with my honorable friend Dr Waldstein at Herculaneum are so important that I think they have some interest for you. My honorable friend, Dr Waldstein, has here realized the methods, he proposed in his immortal work and from that come the highest scientific achievement. We were a staff of 300 scholars and we digged all in the new method, without the old practices of our forefathers. During the excavation, a continuous series of cinematographic photographs has been taken, I regret to be unable to reproduce it. But I can you show any slides.

First slide please.

This slide shows the beautiful site of the city: these wooden houses were the houses of the staff and the 3 thousand workmen; you see the tower, from the height of which my honourable friend Dr Waldstein surveyed personally the excavations.

Next slide please.

This slide shows one of the trenches, you see the elegant and regular masonry, which belong to the best period, middle Oscan three. We spend seven months for studying these beautiful stones; then we made another trench.

Next slide please

This slide shows the end of the second trench, which is more interesting than the first, because it shows a period without masonry. That is one of the period called early Oscan one. In this trench we found beautiful things.

Next slide please

This slide shows a relief of whitish cristallic stone, which the mineralogist of the expedition, my honourable friend Dr Steinkloppe called Marmor. You see the protome of a wife cut in the natural rock. There is no doubt, it is Niobe, she smiles out of archaic clumsiness, but for the rest she mornes the death of her children. The hairs are carved unusually; in reality there are no hairs but snakes and we see the oldest representation of the snake goddess. We found also a later wall-painting representing the same goddess.

Next slide please

The artist of that advanced work characterizes the snakeness of the goddess not by real snakes but all her body is snakely. On the other hand, this picture ressembles some Cretan painting and is interesting for dating the whole.

Next slide

This is the ground plan of the oldest sanctuary of Herculaneum, the oldest because only three stones are in situ. But because we observed the workmen day and night we can say that there was no other stone. All details are sure. To whom was this temple dedicated?

Fortunately we found in the sanctuary a written clay tablet

Next slide

there you see some pictographs. The pictographist of the expedition my honourable friend Dr. Morns reads as follows: Dedicated to Herakles, the founder of this town, the god sitting on his throne with the sacred three and pillar called Herakles standing with his lion-skin. In the deposit of the temple we found a beautiful statuette of this standing Hercules, the Herakles "Orthios"

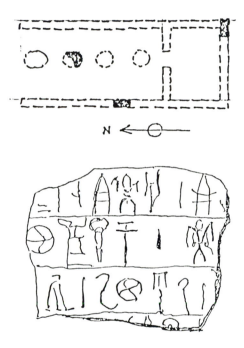

Next slide

Here you see it; it is very naturalistic, you see the lion-skin; the club is long and thin and its end is curved. Another wall painting shows men of Herculaneum worshipping the hero.

Next slide

This picture is of the highest middle Oscan five style. You see the god, and his worshippers throwing fruits in his open mouth. The botanists of the expedition are at variance if they are apples or oranges or lemons.

Next slide

I beg your pardon, I thought there are other slides. Thank you.

Appendix IV

Chairmen and London Staff

CHAIRMEN

(in early years by rotation)
1903–33	G. A. Macmillan
1933–47	J. L. Myres
1947–51	B. Ashmole
1951–59	R. J. H. Jenkins
1959–68	C. M. Robertson
1968–72	V. R. d'A. Desborough
1972–75	N. G. L. Hammond
1975–79	R. A. Higgins
1979–83	P. M. Warren
1983–	R. M. Cook

TREASURERS AND HONORARY TREASURERS
1886–1905	W. Leaf (Hon.)
1905–55	V. W. Yorke (Hon.)
1951–66	H. E. Kneen
1959–68	M. Baird (Hon.)
1966–71	O. Meyer
1969–77	Stacy Waddy (Hon.)
1971–	C. R. G. Stevens

LONDON SECRETARIES

1886–98	G. A. Macmillan (also acted for W. Loring 1899–1901, absent on Active Service)
1898–1903	W. Loring
1903	J. ff. Baker Penoyre, intermittently until 1920
1911–20	Acting, C. A. Hutton
1920–6	M. S. Thompson
1927–30, 1931–34	W. R. Lefanu
1930–31	B. S. Page
1934–7	R. D. Barnett
1937–62	E. Clay
1962–73	M. J. Thornton
1973–5	S. Meade
1975–80	S. Bicknell
1980–	S. E. Waywell

Appendix V

Directors, Assistant Directors, Knossos Curators and Fellows, Athens Secretaries

DIRECTORS

1886–7	F. C. Penrose
1887–95	E. A. Gardner
1895–7	C. Harcourt Smith
1897–1900	D. G. Hogarth
1900–06	R. C. Bosanquet
1906–13	R. M. Dawkins
1913–23	A. J. B. Wace
1923–9	A. M. Woodward
1929–36	H. G. G. Payne
1936	A. Blakeway
1936–46	G. M. Young
1946–54	J. M. Cook
1954–62	M. S. F. Hood
1962–7	A. H. S. Megaw
1967–71	P. M. Fraser
1971–	H. W. Catling

ASSISTANT DIRECTORS, LIBRARIANS

1897	G. C. Richards, for four months
1899	R. C. Bosanquet, for one year
1901	Senior Student, M. N. Tod
1902–5	M. N. Tod
1905	Librarian for one year F. W. Hasluck
1906–10, 1911–15	F. W. Hasluck
1910–11	A. M. Woodward, Acting Assistant Director during Hasluck's leave of absence
1920–23	S. Casson
1923–33	W. A. Heurtley
1933	R. H. Jenkins, Senior Student
1934	A. H. S. Megaw, Senior Student and Librarian
1935–6	A. H. S. Megaw
1936–46	T. J. Dunbabin; from 1939 Deputy Director

1946   H. Thomas, Librarian
1947–8   V. R. d'A Desborough
1948–9   Joint Senior Students and Librarians: P. E. Corbett, R. V. Nicholls
1949–50   M. S. F. Hood
1950–2   P. O. A. Sherrard
1952–5   J. Boardman
1955–6   W. L. Brown
1956–8   G. L. Huxley
1958–61   P. O. A. Sherrard
1962–3   L. H. Sackett
1963–70   M. R. Popham
1970–2   P. M. Warren
1972–6   R. L. N. Barber
1976–9   C. B. Mee
1979–82   A. J. Spawforth
1982–4   F. P. R. Just
1984–   J. A. MacGillivray

KNOSSOS CURATORS AND FELLOWS

1926–9   D. Mackenzie
1929–34   J. D. S. Pendlebury
1934–47   R. W. Hutchinson
1947–52   R. de Jong
1962–3   M. S. F. Hood, Honorary Curator
1977   R. J. Howell, Knossos Fellow
1977–80   J. Carington-Smith, Knossos Fellow
1980–84   J. A. MacGillivray, Curator
1984–   A. A. D. Peatfield, Curator

ATHENS SECRETARIES

(None recorded until 1932)
1932   Part-time R. Woodley
1936–46   Full-time R. Woodley
1946–49   S. Apostolidou
1949–50   G. de la Gardie
1950–75   J. Rabnett, she later became Mrs. Young
1975–76   S. Meade
1976–78   H. Turner
1978–   H. Clark (Efthymiadi)

Appendix VI

Editors of BSA: Supplementary Volumes

EDITORS

1895–1909   C. Harcourt Smith
1904, 1906–26   C. A. Hutton (Assistant Ed. and Joint Ed.)
1922–33   M. Culley
1934–9   T. C. Skeat
1939–45   C. M. Robertson
1946–51   T. J. Dunbabin
1951–6   R. J. Hopper
1956–61   L. H. Jeffery
1961–70   R. J. Hopper
1970–4   J. N. Coldstream
1974–8   R. J. Hopper
1978–   R. A. Tomlinson

SUPPLEMENTARY VOLUMES

1.	*Unpublished Objects from Palaikastro*, R. C. Bosanquet & R. M. Dawkins	1923
2.	*Fortetsa*, J. K. Brock	1957
3.	*The technique of Greek Sculpture*, S. Adam	1966
4.	*Tocra 1963–5: the Archaic Deposits* I, J. Boardman & J. Hayes	1966
5.	*Saliagos: Neolithic Settlement*, J. Evans & C. Renfrew	1968
6.	*Chios: Greek Emporio*, J. Boardman	1967
7.	*Myrtos: Early Bronze Age Settlement*, P. M. Warren	1972
8.	*Knossos: the Sanctuary of Demeter*, J. N. Coldstream	1973
9.	*The Finlay Papers: a Catalogue*, J. M. Hussey	1973
10.	*Tocra, Archaic Deposits* II, *and later Deposits*, J. Boardman & J. Hayes	1974
11.	*Lefkandi* I: The Iron Age, M. R. Popham, L. H. Sackett & P. Themelis	1979/80
12.	*Excavations at Mycenae 1939–1955*, ed. E. B. French	1980
13.	*Knossos: the Bronze Age Palace, plans & sections*, M. S. F. Hood and W. Taylor	1981
14.	*An Archaeological Survey of the Knossos Area*, M. S. F. Hood & David Smyth	1981
15, 16.	*Chios: Prehistoric Emporio and Ayio Gala* I & II, M. S. F. Hood	1981/2
17.	*The Minoan Unexplored Mansion at Knossos*, M. R. Popham	1984/5
18.	*The Archaeology of Cult: the Shrine at Phylakopi*, C. Renfrew	1985

Appendix VII

Visiting Fellows

1952/3	N. G. L. Hammond
1953/4	F. E. Adcock
1954/5	A. W. Gomme
1955/6	H. T. Wade-Gery
1956/7	A. Andrewes
1957/8	C. M. Robertson
1958/9	R. J. Hopper
1959/60	B. Ashmole
1960/1	V. R. d'A. Desborough
1961/2	D. H. F. Gray
1962/3	L. H. Jeffery
1963/4	D. Talbot Rice
1964/5	J. K. Brock
1965/6	R. M. Cook
1966/7	A. W. Lawrence
1967/8	L. H. Sackett
1968/9	R. A. Higgins
1969/70	R. Meiggs
1970/1	F. H. Stubbings
1971/2	J. N. Coldstream
1972/3	G. L. Huxley
1973/4	V. M. Hankey
1974/5	R. A. Tomlinson
1975/6	A. M. Snodgrass
1977/8	J. M. Cook
1978/9	J. T. Killen
1979/80	P. M. Fraser
1980/1	M. S. F. Hood
1981/2	J. K. Anderson
1982/3	J. H. Betts
1983/4	J. K. Campbell
1984/5	Rev. W. Meany
1985/6	W. G. Forrest

Index

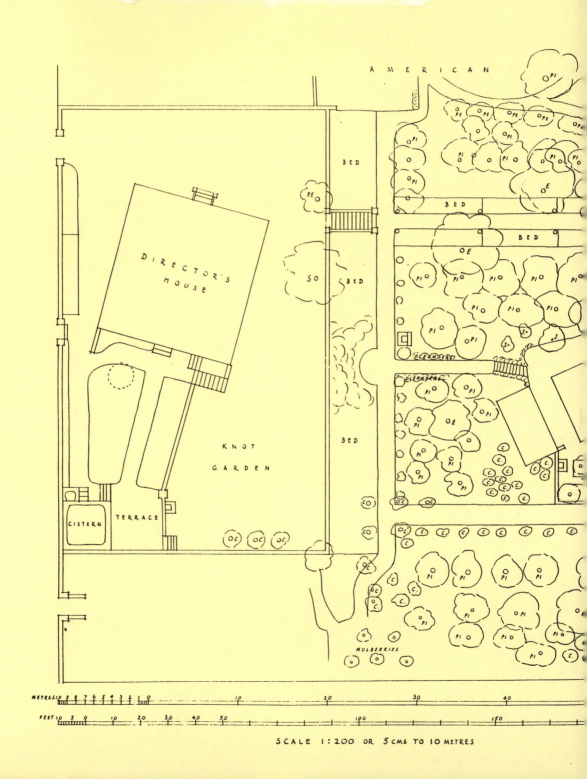

BRITISH SCH
GARD

AMERICAN

DIRECTOR'S HOUSE

BED

BED

BED

BED

BED

KNOT GARDEN

BED

CISTERN

TERRACE

MULBERRIES